Everything
is all right

Everything
is all right

Devotionals at the Crossroads to Eternity

Robert Hasley

invite
PRESS

Plano, Texas

Everything Is All Right:
Devotionals at the Crossroads to Eternity

Everything
is all right

Foreword

Christ-centered, biblically based, grace-filled—this was Robert Hasley—always. After receiving his diagnosis in April 2021, he was understandably dismayed for a day or two while we took our usual morning walk but then returned to the person we all know: our faithful, good shepherd. From that moment on, Robert devoted his time to looking forward. We all miss him deeply. However, the Robert we know still comforts and encourages us when we need it the most.

As Robert reminded us often in the words of Psalm 23:4: "Yea, though I walk through the valley of the shadow of death, I will fear no evil: for thou art with me; thy rod and thy staff they comfort me" (KJV). We were blessed that he shared his thoughts, prayers, and devotions with us during the last fifteen months of his life. They are here in this book for us to thoughtfully remember during the rest of our lives and in times of stress and trouble. We can be sure that today Robert would add the following:

I know everything is all right because—

- by prioritizing my wife, my family, and my friends, I was able to draw strength and love, grace, and hope when I needed it most.

- by focusing on Scripture, I was able to remind myself that I was in good hands and did not have to worry.

- by remembering all the interactions with my congregation and other believers, I could remember that all would be well with my soul.

- I was able to be as productive/helpful to others as they were to me.

- I learned to allow myself to feel the love and grace that God offers us all if we will but accept it.

- I was able to communicate to my family and loved ones how much they mean to me and how much I value them.

- I was ready to accept the place God had prepared for me and await the glorious reunification with my loved ones.

I was blessed to be with Robert the day before he passed away. As he held my hand, he smiled and reminded me several times "It's all right." That was Robert.

Robert lived by the words of Jesus from John 5:24: "Verily, verily, I say unto you, he that heareth my word and believeth on him that sent me, hath everlasting life and shall not come into condemnation, but is passed from death unto life" (KJV). This book is given to us by Robert with grace and his passionate love for God, for life, and for us all.

Bill Warren
with Beverly Warren and John Bailey
Plano, Texas | January 2023

... because of the love
of the family of faith

**"And they came, bringing to Jesus a broken man
in need of healing, carried by four faithful friends."**

Mark 2:3

The story of Jesus healing the paralytic is one of my favorite stories in all of Scripture. Here is an individual who is broken—physically, emotionally, and spiritually—whose friends love him enough to do everything in their power to help him be made whole again. The friends are willing to carry the paralytic as far as necessary to place him in front of a divine healer named Jesus. Then, when their efforts seem doomed to failure due to the crowded home where Jesus is preaching and healing, through sheer determination motivated by unbridled compassion, they find another way to get their friend the help he needs. They make an opening in the roof above and lower the bed on which their friend lays directly in front of Jesus. Because of the steadfast faith of those four companions and their boundless love for their friend, the paralytic is made whole again.

As I have wrestled over the past few weeks with the news of an aggressive cancer invading my body, I have periodically experienced physical, emotional, and spiritual brokenness. My wife Sharon and I have had difficulty comprehending and processing the implications of this news, much less initiating the actions required to tackle the problem. We have, like many of you who have faced similar news personally or in your family, often felt somewhat paralyzed and unable to move forward. That is bad news. The good news has been that hundreds of our friends who are a part of our family of faith have lifted us up and carried us forward when we have not had the strength or energy ourselves.

I think of this Scripture text I received from a church friend on the day we informed our church staff and the congregation about my diagnosis. Fear of an uncertain future for my family and me weighed heavily on my mind that day until I read his text, which contained his version of Isaiah 41:10 ESV:

> Fear not, for I am with you;
> be not dismayed, for I am your God.
> I will strengthen you and help you.
> I will uphold you with my victorious right hand.

Sharing this text, my friend lifted me up and placed me in front of the Lord God Almighty. The Lord then touched me with the power of his grace-filled word, diminishing my fear and replacing it with energizing faith and hope.

Through the power of a song composed by Taylor Davis for the Sunday worship service following my health challenge announcement, both Sharon and I felt uplifted and placed before the Lord by the prayerful sounds of the piano and cello. We experienced God's presence deep in our souls because of the faith, love, and compassion of a composer and two fabulous instrumentalists, Dr. Jonathan Gregoire and Craig Leffer. We felt at that moment a spiritual wholeness in the midst of our vulnerability.

We have also received hundreds of texts, emails, and cards, which have brought smiles to our faces and filled our hearts with joy. The phrase "we are praying for you" has taken on a new power in our lives. We both have found these words reassuring, knowing that we are not alone. They bring us hope that the Lord will use this challenging time to make us all stronger in our faith and inspire us to be more determined than ever to be the passionate servants of Christ that we are all created and called to be.

... because of the **divine gift** of **laughter**

> "Then our mouth was filled with laughter, and our tongue with shouts of joy; then they said among the nations, 'The LORD has done great things for them.'"
>
> Psalm 126:2 NRSV

Faced with a life-threatening cancer diagnosis, I began to prioritize how I would spend each precious moment. I promptly purchased an airline ticket to Virginia to see my granddaughters, daughter-in-law, and youngest son. Upon arrival at the Richmond Airport, I spotted my five-year-old granddaughter, Emogene, and her mom, Amanda. Laughing and smiling, Emogene ran up to me declaring, "I surprised you that I am here to meet you, didn't I, Papaw?" We hugged and laughed as we embarked on a phenomenal weekend of smiles and laughter.

During my stay, I made a live guest appearance on Episode 3 of "Baseball Hall of Fame Jokes with Emogene." This captivating five minutes of Baseball Hall of Fame Jokes was produced by Amanda and Emogene to bring a smile to my face along with anyone else who dared to listen. From personal experience, I can tell you their effort has worked wonderfully. The following are examples of a few of the uplifting jokes that have been told:

Amanda: How is a baseball team similar to a pancake?
Emogene: They both need a good batter!

Amanda: What did the baseball glove say to the baseball when they said goodbye?
Emogene: Catch you later!

Amanda: What is a baseball player's least favorite *Star Wars* movie?
Emogene: The Umpire Strikes Back!

Add a drumroll, bells, and Emogene's giggles, and you can imagine what a treat this moment is every Friday. For me, this moment is a far more effective treatment for what ails me than any medicine I have or will ever take. As the psalmist said, "The Lord does do great things for us through the gift of laughter."

. . . because we can do **hard things**

> "Father, if you are willing, remove this cup from me.
> Nevertheless, not my will, but yours be done."
>
> Luke 22:42 ESV

On a table in the entry hall to my son Will's and daughter-in-law Amanda's home is a wooden photo frame with the following quotation: "We Can Do Hard Things." In the middle of facing an unwanted medical diagnosis, this caught my attention. My thoughts carried me to the biblical scene of the Garden of Gethsemane where Jesus prayerfully agonized over a very difficult decision he had to make. He could either run from the chief priests and temple guards who were about to capture him, torture him, and hang him on a cross for what they believed to be numerous heretical words and actions, or he could stand his ground and fulfill his role as the prophet Isaiah's long-awaited "suffering servant" who had come to redeem the world from the power of fear and death. Jesus, in conversation with the Lord God Almighty, made his choice to give up his life and offer a life of hope, joy, and love to a broken world.

Memorial Day weekend reminds us of those in the U.S. Armed Forces who stood their ground to defend our lives and liberties. Like Jesus, the cost of doing the hard thing cost them their lives in order that others might live. My Uncle Robert, who flew reconnaissance missions in the South Pacific during World War II; my Uncle Austin, who flew "The Hump" in order to deliver supplies to our allies while battling Japanese fighters during WWII; and my father-in-law, Bill, who fought with the 3rd Army at the Battle of the Bulge under the command of General Patton, were all willing to risk their lives for a higher calling and purpose, knowing that every moment of every day the Lord God Almighty was watching over them and their families back home.

None of us can avoid dealing with difficult situations in this life. When hard things confront us, our faith calls upon us to face those hard things and not to turn away. Our faith challenges us to focus on the purpose that the Lord God Almighty placed upon us on this earth: to love the Lord our God with all our heart, mind, soul, and strength and to love our neighbor as ourselves. In so doing, we find a way to build God's kingdom on earth as it is in heaven, even when the challenges before us threaten to prevent us from staying the course. The grace that the Lord offers us to keep our focus is the knowledge that we are never alone in our work and mission. God is with us, and our family of faith embodies God's never-ending love and compassion to walk beside us.

... because of the small things that bring great joy

"Complete my joy by being of the same mind, having the same love, being in full accord and of one mind."

Philippians 2:2 ESV

Upon arrival in Virginia just after my unanticipated medical diagnosis, when my granddaughter Emogene and her mom met me at the airport to drive me to their home in Crozet, Emogene ran up to me, gave me a big hug, and told me that she and her family had planned a big surprise for me. I figured that I would be able to get her to spill the beans about the big surprise during the 90-minute trip to her house. However, I was wrong. The next day, I still couldn't persuade her to reveal the surprise. Then, on the third day, Emogene ran into my room to let me know that it was time to get into the car so I could go to see my big surprise.

We got into the car with my son Will and daughter-in-law Amanda, and drove a few blocks from the house. Then, we took a sharp left turn into the newly built automated car wash in Crozet. As a matter of fact, this was the first and only automated car wash in this tiny town outside of Charlottesville, Virginia. We lined up behind two other cars to wait while Emogene informed me about this amazing car wash. Slowly, we rolled upon the track that took us into the wash. A buzzer and flashing red light notified us to stop the car.

Then, the yelling and screaming began led by Emogene and parroted by her two-year-old sister Joy. "Papaw," they yelled, "Can you believe it?" Red, blue, and green lights began to flash as the body of the car was sprayed with water. Then, when the rainbow-colored soap was splattered on the windshield and on every other part of the vehicle, the screaming and yelling from my precious granddaughters was much louder but was like sweet music to my ears. Why? Their great joy in a small, simple, and common event that takes place millions of times every minute around the world filled my heart with hope that joy is everywhere around us, especially in small, unexpected places.

Ever since returning from my visit to Crozet where my big surprise—a visit with my granddaughters to an automated car wash—brought great joy to my heart, I have been searching for joy in the small things. The more I look, the more joy I seem to find. I have found great joy in looking through old family photo albums that I assembled many years ago. I have received great joy from holding my wife's hand as we fall asleep in bed at night. I have discovered great joy Facetiming my loved ones more frequently. These are all small things. However, what I have come to realize through Emogene and even the Lord God Almighty, who found great joy in the small things, like walking and talking with Adam and Eve in the Garden of Eden, is that, if we are together being of the same mind and having the same love, our joy is surprisingly and divinely complete.

... because God is God and we are not

"For all things are possible with God."

Mark 10:27 ESV

When I was first diagnosed a few weeks ago with aggressive cancer, my feelings of fear and helplessness were evident in my futile attempts to gain a sense of control. I challenged the doctor's diagnosis and instead turned to self-diagnosing. On one occasion when my arm started to swell, I diagnosed my injury as some stretched tendons in my left arm due to swinging a golf club. During my weekly visit to my doctor, he asked why I had not notified him about this swelling. I emphatically told him that it was nothing but strained muscles from swinging a golf club. He quickly countered my diagnosis, informing me that I had a blood clot that needed to be treated promptly with medication. Then he respectfully but firmly reminded me that he was the doctor, and I was not.

Over my lifetime, God has reminded me on many occasions, either through Scripture or experience, that God is God, and I am not. Like my doctor, who saved me from a life-threatening stroke, God manages to save us again and again from life-diminishing decisions that arise out of our need to control rather than our need to have faith in God's unlimited possibilities. As I have worked the past few weeks to place my life, both present and future, in God's hands, I have begun to experience grace upon grace. When I turn to God for help to make each day a meaningful and joyful experience regardless of how I physically or emotionally feel, I experience tremendous gratitude that I am not alone in this world. God has not finished using my God-given gifts to build the kingdom of God on earth as it is in heaven. Placing my life in God's hands has given me hope that all things are possible with God. Depending only on faith in myself, I diminish my life and limit my possibilities through loving service to make this world a more grace-filled place to live, work, and play.

My sincere prayer is that you will join me on a spiritual journey to let go of the need to control and let faith in God, as revealed in Jesus Christ, guide your life.

. . . because we have a Shepherd who guides us in this life and the life to come

"For the Lamb in the midst of the throne will be their shepherd, and he will guide them to springs of living water, and God will wipe away every tear from their eyes."

Revelation 7:17 ESV

Over the years, I have turned to Psalm 23 as a source of strength and assurance during the most challenging times of my life. The knowledge that the same Lord God Almighty who created us is also present to guide us throughout our life journey brings me a peace beyond understanding. The author of Psalm 23 has found that peace in his relationship with his Lord who serves as his Creator and Guide. My prayer is that sharing his psalm will bring you a divine, lasting peace deep within your soul.

> The LORD is my shepherd; I shall not want.
> He makes me lie down in green pastures.
> He leads me beside still waters.
> He restores my soul.
> He leads me in paths of righteousness
> for his name's sake.

Even though I walk through the valley of the shadow of death, I will fear no evil, for you are with me; your rod and your staff they comfort me. You prepare a table before me in the presence of my enemies; you anoint my head with oil; my cup overflows. Surely goodness and mercy shall follow me all the days of my life, and I shall dwell in the house of the LORD forever. (Psalm 23:1-6 ESV)

. . . because the church embodies the faith and love of Christ

> "Therefore, we ourselves boast about you in the churches of God for your steadfastness and faith."

2 Thessalonians 1:4 ESV

Today, Reverend Arthur Jones officially assumed the role as Senior Pastor of St. Andrew United Methodist Church as appointed by the North Texas Conference of The United Methodist Church. In addition, Arthur has graciously asked me to serve on staff in the role of Founding Pastor, focusing upon building a ministry with retirees and those approaching retirement. The bishop has chosen to appoint me to St. Andrew to fulfill this role as established by Arthur.

Like the Apostle Paul in his letter to the Thessalonians, I am about to boast to you about the faith and love of Arthur Jones. Arthur is an ordained elder in The United Methodist Church who has dedicated himself to serving as a faithful servant of a loving Christ. We at St. Andrew have all seen Arthur's deep faith in Jesus Christ as he boldly and passionately communicates the truth of Christ through his preaching in a way that engages our minds and transforms our hearts. We have also seen the size of his heart for all of God's people as he has, over eleven years, compassionately shepherded us through difficult times and celebrated with us during good times. Under Arthur's leadership, the future of St. Andrew could not be brighter. Furthermore, I could not be more excited about Arthur's vision for the many ways that St. Andrew can make an impact for Christ over the next decades. Arthur truly embodies the faith and love of Christ.

Now, I want to boast about you, the St. Andrew family. More than thirty-five years ago, I was groomed by Dr. Leighton Farrell, the Senior Pastor at Highland Park United Methodist Church, to found a new United Methodist church in Plano. I was then appointed by Bishop John Russel. I remember feeling excitement for the opportunity and then experiencing pure terror at the tremendous weight of the task of building something from nothing. In short order, the courageous and dedicated volunteers who gathered around to build our church convinced me that, if our new church named St. Andrew was going to get off the ground, I needed to realize that *I* was not founding a new church; instead, *we* were founding a new church.

As I look back over thirty-five years of serving alongside thousands of faithful founders of St. Andrew, I do not remember a time when you, the St. Andrew family, did not rise to the occasion to help build a church of faith and love, seeking to be all that God has created us to be. Many of you made significant personal sacrifices to build God's kingdom here on earth as it is in heaven. We would not be the church we are today without you choosing to serve as the embodiment of Christ's faith and love. Therefore, my prayer is that, when Arthur writes his letter (prayerfully more than thirty-five years from now), he will boast about you just as I am boasting about you today, writing that you stepped up every time your church needed you to build God's kingdom of faith and love. By the way, you do not have to teach Arthur that the pronoun *we* best describes St. Andrew. He already knows because you have taught him this over the past eleven years. Arthur is clearly a faster learner than I am.

I, an all-too-often struggling servant of Jesus Christ, wish you peace, and that God's hand might be not only on our faith family but also on me through you. My soul feels the touch of your grace-filled hands and prayers. You are the best! Thank you!

. . . because we are **blessed** with the **gift** to create **memories**

> "For everything there is a season,
> and a time for every matter under heaven:
> a time to be born, and a time to die;
> a time to plant, and a time to pluck up what is planted,
> . . . a time by God's grace to create memories,
> and a time to joyfully recall those memories."

The last verse is a personal addition in the spirit of Ecclesiastes 3:1-8

I believe that the ability to create loving memories is a God-given gift, and that investing in creating those memories serves to help us hold onto those we love far beyond even death itself. Therefore, in the midst of my own battle with cancer, I have recently been on a mission to create such divine memories. In the process of investing in relationships with those I love, I have had the privilege to experience a number of firsts:

- I took my first trip with my two-year-old and five-year-old granddaughters, Joy and Emogene, to Six Flags Over Texas. With the blessing of my son Will, daughter-in-law Amanda, and daughter Erin, I rode with Emogene on her first roller coaster ride. We screamed on the downward trajectory while holding tightly onto one another.

- I took my first trip to a phenomenally beautiful section of Montana to hear my son Stephen's and daughter-in law Amanda's dreams of one day living and raising a family there. The happiness in their hearts and the smiles on their faces brought tremendous joy to my soul. There, I also experienced the first of witnessing with my son and daughter-in-law a herd of wild horses crossing a Montana range. Then, on our last day, we spotted a rare, great gray owl flying silently and gracefully across a meadow.

- I participated in my first Fourth of July neighborhood parade with my six-month-old granddaughter Aashni, my daughter-in-law Ananya, her parents, and my son John. It was a perfect day filled with love, laughter, and gratitude for a nation that strives to make sacrifices for liberty and justice for all. The wonder and curiosity in Aashni's eyes and the smile on Aashni's face will stay with me always.

- For our anniversary, I gave Sharon a gift that was for me a first. I gave her something that she was to open and then give back to me. The gift was my wedding ring threaded onto an attractive necklace. Since my cancer treatment has resulted in some swelling of my ring finger, I wanted to make sure I could still wear my wedding ring. I thought wearing it close to my heart would be appreciated by Sharon. It was.

As you can readily ascertain, the essence of creating lasting memories is the love you invest in those you care about. For me and for you, that investment is possible because God first loved us; Christ's unconditional love for us is what makes possible the creation of lasting, loving relationship memories. What memory, by the grace of God, will you take the time and make the effort to create today?

... because we have **each other**

"This is my commandment, that you love one another
as I have loved you."

John 15:12 NRSV

I recall a time in late December when one of our St. Andrew adult Sunday school classes showed up *en masse* to
visit a member in the hospital who was in the latter stages
of her battle with cancer. Class members expressed their
love for her and her husband and then proceeded to sing
Christmas carols, the sound of which echoed throughout
the hospital.

During my forty-five years in ministry, I have come
to believe that there are angels among us, and those angels
are individuals who know God loves them and who celebrate that divine love by loving their neighbors in words
and actions. I have been surrounded by angels ever since
my cancer diagnosis in late April. They have provided
transformative strength and hope throughout my journey.

The musical group Alabama sang a song entitled "Angels Among Us" that succinctly captures the difference
that angels (God's messengers) make in our lives. The following lyrics I leave with you, as written by Becky Hobbs
and Don Goodman:

Oh, I believe there are angels among us.
Sent down to us, from somewhere up above.[1]

[1] Becky Hobbs and Don Goodman, "Angels Among Us,"
https://www.youtube.com/watch?v=y_4Xfj2LRSA.

... because of God's gift of a second chance

"And Jesus said, 'Father, forgive them, for they know not what they do.'"

Luke 23:34 ESV

Our brokenness as human beings is highlighted in the fall of humanity as recorded in the first few chapters of the book of Genesis. In a nutshell, the message of Genesis warns us that our self-centeredness serves to separate us from God, one another, and even from ourselves as God created us to be. Therefore, sin is the state of being separated from God, others, and self.

The good news of the gospel is that the consequences of sin—which ultimately lead to isolation, enmity toward others, and a diminished life—do not have to be lasting. Jesus Christ modeled from the cross that the Lord God Almighty is the Lord of second chances and more. God's love is unconditional. Though we often make choices that separate us from God, God through Christ remains faithful to us for all eternity.

I told a story some time ago about an interaction I experienced with my father. We had a fundamental disagreement about my college choice, and I said some things that were self-centered and harmful to our relationship. I regretted my words immediately after they left my mouth, and I feared that damage had been done that I could not undo. I flew home after my first year of college (the college that my dad preferred) to enroll in a new college. Arriving home, I walked off the airplane expecting my mom to be there to greet me at the airport. To my great surprise, my father was waiting there to welcome me home and insisted upon carrying my luggage to the car. From that day forward, I knew nothing would ever diminish our love for each other.

The cross revealed that nothing (even sin itself) will ultimately ever separate us from the love of God as revealed in Christ Jesus our Lord. Therefore, we can boldly proclaim no matter the circumstance that in Christ "Everything Is All Right."

... because **darkness** is always followed by the **dawn**

"And God said, 'Let there be light,'
and there was light."

Genesis 1:3 ESV

During the visit to Crozet following my diagnosis, my five-year-old granddaughter Emogene, two-year-old granddaughter Joy, and I were very active during my stay. Our activities included a hike to a railroad tunnel excavated by an engineer after whom Crozet was named. On our walk to the tunnel, Emogene spotted what looked like a long, black snake. The snake was not moving, so my daughter-in-law Amanda and I decided to walk around it. Emogene was gripped with fear as the snake raised its head and flicked its tongue toward her and us. I felt certain that fear would continue to overwhelm Emogene as we approached the long, dark tunnel entrance.

However, I was wrong. Amanda had brought a flashlight for Emogene. As soon as she turned on the flashlight, the darkness of the tunnel was pierced by the light, revealing a brightly colored frog hopping along the moist floor of the cave. The light immediately dispelled any fear that Emogene had previously felt.

We are told in the book of Genesis that:

> In the beginning . . . the earth was without form and void, and darkness was over the face of the deep. . . . And God said, "Let there be light," and there was light. And God saw that the light was good. And God separated the light from the darkness. God called the light Day, and the darkness he called Night. And there was evening and there was morning, the first day. (Genesis 1:1-5 ESV)

From that moment until now, the darkness of night has always been followed by the light of dawn.

The fact that God created light to break through the darkness gives hope to those who feel trapped in a dark place. May you see God's light in your dark moments and, even more, may you be God's light of hope to someone who is overwhelmed by darkness.

... because of **flashes** of **light**
from **heaven** above

**"The star that the magi had seen went before them
until it came to rest over the place where the child was."**

Matthew 2:9

A little over a week ago my oldest son, Stephen, and I were driving back to Dallas from Fort Worth in the early evening. The skies had grown dark. Suddenly, Stephen cried out, "Look at that!" Streaking through the night sky was a stream of light that transformed into a bright glow before it vanished from the sky. In awe, we both commented that we had never seen anything quite like what we saw that evening. The next day, news posts told of a meteor that had been seen by people across North Texas, which disintegrated in flames some twenty-seven miles above the earth.

When Stephen and I spotted that flash of light coming down from heaven that night, all the problems and concerns that we were nursing were forgotten. The bright light completely seized our attention. I find myself wondering if that was the experience of the wise men when they spotted a star (some biblical historians have suggested they saw a meteor) that led them to Bethlehem and to the Christ Child. If the flash of light from heaven did not make them forget their concerns for themselves and for the world, I believe that seeing the Christ Child did. They saw in him a light from heaven that would overcome the darkness in the world. They would have returned home believing that, now, "everything is all right."

The power of Christ is like a flash of light that, when we see it, will reduce all our worries and concerns through the brightness of its glory.

... because the Lord God places encouragers in our path

"Therefore encourage one another
and build one another up."

1 Thessalonians 5:11 ESV

Upon receiving my unexpected cancer diagnosis, a good friend gifted me a wristband that reads "You Got This." Now, I do not usually wear bracelets or wristbands. I am a wedding ring and watch kind of guy. However, for some reason, I immediately began wearing the wristband, and now I have worn it for three and a half months.

More often than I ever imagined, I look at my band and the words printed on it. I am reminded each time that I have good friends who are with me in my battle with an aggressive cancer. I am also reminded that, along with my friends, the Lord God is with me every step of the way no matter what physical or mental challenges I face each day. With the Lord on my side and good friends encouraging me, I believe with all my heart and mind that "I've got this!"

As I think of the word *encourage,* I am reminded of a definition I ran across some years back: "to hearten or to put one's heart back in place." Whether fighting an illness or facing agonizing circumstances of any kind, it can be rather easy to lose heart. However, I am so very thankful that the Lord God Almighty has seen fit to place people in our lives who give us the heart and courage to face life's challenges with hope. Encouragement from others helps us to handle whatever comes our way. Even more, as people of faith, we have Christ Jesus who spent his three years of ministry encouraging those who had lost hope or lost their way. To a paralytic who was brought before Jesus by encouraging friends, Jesus said, "Take heart" (Matthew 9:2). Then Jesus forgave the paralytic's sins and encouraged him to take up his bed and walk. Jesus offered words of encouragement to a Samaritan woman beside a well in Sychar, and with renewed self-confidence she became the first church planter as she effectively recruited people in her village to follow Christ.

To whom might you offer today a divine encouraging word to build that person up? By doing so, you will be making an impact for Christ.

... because of the divine gift of grit

"I have fought the good fight, I have finished the race, I have kept the faith."

2 Timothy 4:7 NRSV

As I stood by my mom while she battled an aggressive cancer at age 64, I remember thinking that she was facing her battle with an extra helping of the God-given gift of true grit: courage, fortitude, and resolution. She wrote down a list of her favorite Scripture passages, which she placed next to her bed on her nightstand. She turned to them for light and strength during her darker and more difficult days. Mom drew from her deep and abiding faith, displaying the divine gift of grit before a powerful enemy called cancer.

The Scripture passage printed above was part of a letter written by the Apostle Paul as he was awaiting execution. Facing his death, the end of his vital ministry, and abandonment of his followers due to the fear of persecution, Paul was encouraging his spiritual brother Timothy to draw on the grit of Christ Jesus to stand firm in the faith. Paul was urging Timothy to let Christ rule his heart and mind as he faced an uncertain future that would include pain and suffering. In his letter, Paul reminded Timothy that he possessed, through faith, the hope and grit of Christ Jesus, which was revealed when Jesus faced the ridicule of religious leaders. Paul helped Timothy remember that Christ Jesus faced suffering and death on the cross where he chose not to seek revenge upon his persecutors. Christ Jesus chose instead to cry out to God Almighty in prayer, "Father, forgive them for they know not what they do" (Luke 23:34 ESV). The divine characteristics of grit, courage, and fortitude were gifts that Paul hoped to pass on to Timothy and to his followers in the early churches he had planted throughout Asia Minor.

As members of the St. Andrew family who are called upon to be witnesses to the presence of Christ Jesus in our lives, I ask myself and you, "Are we reflecting in our words and deeds the true nature of Christ's grit and courage?" If not, the Lord God Almighty, by the power of his amazing grace, has given us today to begin.

... because of infinite **opportunities** to let **others know** you **care**

"We ought always to give thanks to God for you . . . because your faith is growing abundantly, and the love of every one of you for one another is increasing."

2 Thessalonians 1:3 ESV

Over the years as shepherd of a large, growing church family, I was challenged to find ways to make time to communicate to my immediate family how much I love them. For my boys, I would set aside time to take them to sporting events, and on special occasions, I would give them baseball cards from my childhood collection. I would include a personalized note, highlighting how a star player reminded me of characteristics I saw in them. For my daughter, I made it a priority to attend her school functions and to set up times to take her out to eat where we would catch up on her day. For my wife, who battles chronic health issues, I enjoy times when we listen to our favorite music together, and I like frequently surprising her with a bouquet of flowers specifically chosen as a reminder of a memorable trip or a special moment in our life together.

As I face a battle with an aggressive cancer, the above ways of communicating love to my family have become even more important to me and, therefore, more frequent.

I just returned from a visit with my oldest son, Stephen. What I enjoyed most during our visit were the moments we spent looking through a genealogical album I had put together for each of my children some eleven years ago. The album is filled with photos of grandparents and great-grandparents, along with my handwritten stories about personal memories with them and family. As Stephen and I flipped through the album page by page, I was able to tell him about the special traits and characteristics I witnessed in my parents, grandparents, and great-grandparents that I now see in him. Our time together was an opportunity to communicate with my son how proud I am of him and how much I love him.

Like the Apostle Paul, I give thanks to God daily for the faith I share with my family and for the love between us that is increasing because we make opportunities to express how much we care for one another. My prayer is that, starting today, you will make opportunities to let those around you know how much you care.

... because we **all** have an

eternal purpose

"And Jesus said, 'You shall love the Lord your God with all of your heart and with all of your soul and with all of your mind.' This is the greatest and first commandment. And a second is like it: 'You shall love your neighbor as yourself.'"

Matthew 22:37-39

The Lord God has given all of creation a job to do. Our job consists of building God's kingdom on earth as it is in heaven, which involves loving God and our neighbor as ourselves. However, our kingdom-building work does not end in this life but continues in our eternal life with God. As I face an uphill battle with cancer, there is something reassuring in believing that my divine calling does not end with the last breath I take on this earth but continues as a calling for all of God's children for all of eternity. Just as God will never stop loving us and will never leave our side, we are given the tremendous privilege to never stop loving God and never stop loving our neighbor in this life and in the life to come.

As I listened to the anthem "Open My Eyes That I May See" in worship this past weekend, I heard a personal chal-

---

lenge to open my eyes to the truth of the divine work that we have all been given and to experience the freedom of embracing the daily tasks God gives to us. Hear with me God's call to see, listen, and act in a spirit of love as expressed through God's servant, Clara H. Scott, in 1895:

"Open My Eyes, That I May See"

Open my eyes, that I may see glimpses of truth thou hast for me;
Place in my hands the wonderful key that shall unclasp and set me free.

Refrain
Silently now I wait for thee, ready, my God, thy will to see.
Open my eyes, illumine me, Spirit divine!

Open my ears, that I may hear voices of truth thou sendest clear;
and while the wave-notes fall on my ear, everything false will disappear. *Refrain*

Open my mouth, and let me bear gladly the warm truth everywhere;
open my heart and let me prepare love with thy children thus to share. *Refrain*

... because faith overcomes fear

"For everyone who has been born of God overcomes the world. And this is the victory that has overcome the world—our faith."

1 John 5:4 ESV

I was called to be with a St. Andrew family as they disconnected life support for a beloved husband, father, and grandfather. The grandfather's elementary-aged grandson entered the ICU room and went straight to his bedside. The grandson spoke calmly to his grandfather while playing with his grandfather's ear. His grandfather was not verbally responsive. When the grandchild finished saying what he wanted to say, he kissed his grandad and turned to leave. Just as he reached the door he turned back to his grandfather and with great confidence declared, "Grandad, I will see you in heaven." Then, with a look of peace on his face the grandson walked out the door.

His words touched the heart and soul of everyone in that hospital room.

Some believe that the antonym to the word *faith* is the word *doubt.* Based on my life experiences, including my recent battle with cancer, the antonym to *faith* is actually *fear.* To live in this world is to know the power of fear over our lives. We fear so many things: loss, failure, insignificance, uncertainty, and even success. Yet, I believe our greatest fear is the fear of death.

Scripture teaches us that faith is the only force in this world that can overcome death. However, faith is not something we earn; it is a gift from God that we are invited to accept. Faith is a gift that the elementary child, who confidently told his grandfather that he would see him again in heaven, possessed. Faith is a gift the psalmist received from God, his Shepherd, which prompted him to write: "Even though I walk through the valley of the shadow of death, I will fear no evil, for [the Lord] is with me; [the Lord's] rod and staff, they comfort me" (Psalm 23:4 ESV). Faith is the life-giving, divine gift that the Apostle Paul unwrapped before he wrote:

> Who shall separate us from the love of Christ? . . .
> For I am sure that neither death nor life, nor angels nor rulers, nor things present nor things to come, nor powers, nor height nor depth, nor anything else in all of creation will be able to separate us from the love of God in Christ Jesus our Lord. (Romans 8:35a, 38-39 ESV)

Join me in asking the Lord God to grant you an extra helping of faith to be able to overcome the fear that will confront you today.

. . . when we choose to **invest** in **those** we **love**

"For God so loved the world that he gave his one and only Son, that whoever believes in him should not perish but have eternal life."

John 3:16 NIV

The mother of a friend was diagnosed with a terminal illness. In shock and with deep concern, my friend drove a significant distance as soon as possible to be with her mom and dad. Sleeping in the guest room next to her parents' room, my friend overheard the following interaction between them before they fell asleep.

They both used their communication devices to play for each other their favorite music. Then they began taking turns singing to each other the music that was most meaningful to both. Before finally retiring for the night, their final communication was to say out loud how much they loved each other.

My friend's level of concern over how her parents would deal with this shocking news regarding her mom's illness diminished significantly. As a matter of fact, you might say that, on that night when she heard her parents' loving interaction, she was immediately reassured not only that "everything *would* be all right" but that "everything *is* all right," no matter the outcome.

When a teacher who grew up in a small village called Nazareth was nailed to a cross, his mother stood at the base of that cross grieving her son's fate. Yet Jesus did something totally unexpected while on the cross. While most victims of crucifixion cursed their persecutors, Jesus chose to look up to heaven and have a brief conversation with God. Those who were standing at the foot of the cross heard Jesus pray, "Father, forgive them for they know not what they do" (Luke 23:34 ESV).

Like my friend's parents' loving interaction with one another, the love God and Jesus had for one another and for all their children in that moment was unconditional. It launched a process of healing and hope in a broken world. Is there a conversation you can have with someone this week in which you can communicate divine, unconditional love that will bring them hope and healing? That is the most powerful and effective way (as Jesus demonstrated on the cross) that we can communicate to someone we love that "everything *will be* all right" and, even more, that "everything *is* all right."

...when **investing** in relationships is our **first priority**

"I thank my God always when I remember you
in my prayers, because I hear of your love
and of the faith that you have toward the Lord Jesus
and for all of the saints."

Philemon 1:4-5 ESV

Several years ago, I signed up for a three-day silent spiritual retreat at a Catholic retreat center. I was feeling overwhelmed in several areas of my life and thought this might serve as a helpful spiritual discipline to free me from that which was weighing me down. Surprisingly, my breakthrough moment came on a visit to a nearby cemetery. In silence, I walked from headstone to headstone reading the inscriptions. I immediately realized that I could see no inscription mentioning the deceased's net worth or accumulated assets. Instead, every inscription referred to a significant relationship or relationships such as "Devoted Follower of Christ" or "Beloved Husband, Wife, Father, Mother, Brother, Sister, or Friend."

Much of what once was so overwhelming in my life involved to-do lists at work and at home. My trip to the cemetery opened my eyes to the fact that my priorities were out of balance. I was spending an inordinate amount of time on administrative details that were draining me spiritually, intellectually, and emotionally. I left that cemetery with a commitment to spend more of my time and energy investing in the relationships that energized and encouraged me and enabled me to do the same for others. My more balanced approach to my daily routine brought more joy and less stress into my life.

When I was diagnosed with an aggressive cancer, my first thought was to tackle several administrative details that needed my attention. However, I paused and remembered the inscriptions on those headstones in the little country cemetery bordering the Catholic retreat center. I did proceed to tackle administrative work that needed to be addressed following my diagnosis, but I balanced that work by investing in relationships with family and friends. Investing in those relationships has brought tremendous joy and energy to my heart and soul. As a matter of fact, investing in relationships is the pathway to finding true love, joy, meaning, and hope in this life, no matter the challenges facing us. What investments might you make today in the people who intersect your life? What investment might you make today in your relationship with Jesus Christ?

... when we choose to **hold hands**

"I am with you always, to the end of the age."

Matthew 28:20 ESV

Hand-holding is a cherished tradition in the Hasley household. My wife, Sharon, and I hold hands at night when our heads hit the pillow. We often interlace our fingers when we listen to our favorite music. We clasp hands as we walk to the car together. After we received the results from my recent biopsy, Sharon and I sat and held hands for a while in silence.

For me, holding hands is a powerful reminder that we are not alone in this world. There is a strength that comes from facing life's challenges hand in hand with another person. Hand-holding is a concrete expression of steadfast love. As a matter of fact, I believe that we were created by the Lord God to do life together with God and one another. Holding hands to pray or to show that we care is a visible affirmation of that belief.

Recently, my nine-month-old granddaughter, Aashni, grabbed my fingers and pulled herself up from sitting to a standing position. You should have seen the smile on her face. Handholding has a way of lifting us up in our times of need. By the power of God's grace, find someone to lift up today, and you will be divinely blessed by being lifted up in the process.

... when you **value** above all else
your **friends**

> **"Greater love has no one than this:**
> **to lay down one's life for one's friends."**
>
> John 15:13 NIV

The first true hero I remember meeting as a child was my Great-Uncle Tiny Bryan. He was diagnosed with polio at a very early age. Due to his illness, he lost his ability to walk without the use of leg braces and crutches. My Grandmother Stephens turned to me one day and declared, "You may not know this, but your Great-Uncle Bryan is a hometown hero. One day he went to Lake Gurdon with friends and, while sitting on the shore, he noticed that one of his friends was flailing and gasping for air in the middle of the lake. Great-Uncle Bryan left his crutches and braces on the shore. He then used only his upper-body strength to swim to his drowning friend and pull him to shore. He saved his friend's life that day. Now, when people see your Great-Uncle Bryan, they do not see him as someone who is physically challenged because of a terrible disease; instead, they see him as someone who, out of love, risked his own life to save the life of a friend."

Likewise, when I think of our crucified and risen Christ, I do not think of a victim of a horrific beating and torturous death on a cross. Rather, I think of a loving, merciful, grace-filled Christ who did whatever was necessary to save humankind from drowning in a sea of fear, sin, and death. As a matter of fact, Great-Uncle Bryan was a man of deep faith who believed God through Christ had created him to help build God's kingdom here on earth as it is in heaven. He chose to be God's kingdom builder by choosing to risk his life to save a friend. What are we willing to risk to be God's kingdom builders this week?

... when **compassion** emanates from our **pain**

> "For I wrote to you out of much affliction and anguish of heart and with many tears, not to cause you pain but to let you know the abundant love that I have for you."
>
> 2 Corinthians 2:4 ESV

God gives each of us a choice as to how we respond to the pain we experience during our lifetime. We can focus our energy on blaming who or what we believe to be the cause of our suffering. We can choose to assume the victim role by asking "Why me?" and dwelling on the unfairness of life. Or we can choose the response of the Apostle Paul to his own personal anguish. Paul wrote a letter expressing compassion to followers of Christ who were experiencing their own personal pain.

Six months ago, when I received a diagnosis of an aggressive cancer, I initially responded in negative ways. Out of anger, I sought to blame something or someone. Then my fear and anxiety led me to a dark place of self-pity. However, the words of the Apostle Paul helped me to move to a better place, or more specifically, a spiritually healthier place. As a follower of Christ, Paul knew that, amidst the agony of crucifixion, Jesus chose to speak words of compassion from the cross rather than spew words of condemnation or bitterness for his circumstances. When confronted with his own affliction, Paul chose to travel the same road taken by Jesus.

Therefore, inspired by Paul, I have intentionally spent the last few months reaching out to others who are battling cancer or the effects of chemo treatments. I have a chemo buddy now whose empathy and compassion have made my own cancer journey much easier, both spiritually and emotionally. I do not believe God inflicts us with pain. However, I do believe that by the power of divine, amazing grace, the Lord God gives us an opportunity to respond to our pain with acts of empathy and compassion directed toward the afflicted. Name someone in your life who could use an extra helping of compassion and contact that person today.

. . . when we have a **purpose**

> **"For God so loved the world that he gave his only Son,
> that whoever believes in him should not perish but
> have eternal life."**
>
> John 3:16 ESV

A few years back, I received a phone call from a former student of mine, Curt, who was a member of the University Class at Highland Park United Methodist Church. I was the pastor and teacher of the class during the time Curt was at Southern Methodist University (SMU). Now 50 years old, Curt called to ask me to visit him in the hospital. With the shades drawn, his hospital room was extremely dark, which matched Curt's state of mind. He told me that he had been diagnosed with a rare form of terminal cancer. Since then, he had drifted away from a relationship with Christ, which he regretted. He said he had contacted me so that I might pray with him. He wanted the assurance that God would be with him as he battled his cancer. We prayed together that evening.

When I walked into Curt's hospital room the next day, light was shining brightly through the open blinds. I was immediately reminded of Genesis 1:3: "And God said, 'Let there be light,' and there was light." However, there was not only light in the room. A light shone in Curt's eyes that had not been there the night before during our visit. That light was clearly God's presence. God's presence was confirmed and revealed when Curt spoke to me about two decisions he had made after we prayed. First, he had decided to donate his body for research. His cancer was uncommon, and he felt that medical researchers might be able to help others by studying his cancer after his death. Second, as someone who had chosen to remain single, Curt did not have heirs to whom he could leave his estate. He had prayed about it and decided to help his sibling who had two children who would soon be faced with applying to and paying for college. He decided to leave his niece and nephew enough money so that they would be able to attend the college of their choice.

The dramatic change that had taken place in that hospital room was twofold. First, the transformation from darkness to light was for me a visible witness that the light of God's love permeated that hospital room. Second, wherever God is, he is at work carrying out his purpose to show us the way to love God by loving and serving our neighbor. Curt, through the donation of his body to research and his choice to help his niece and nephew afford a quality education, was honoring God by providing for the needs of his neighbors and family. Curt had an aura of assurance that day that told me that he knew God was present and that God's love had opened Curt's eyes to his purpose while he still had breath in his lungs. If he were here today, Curt would tell you that he had the honor during the last few months of his life to help build God's kingdom of love here on earth as it is in heaven.

Reflect with me for a moment on your God-given purpose. If you are uncertain about your purpose, turn to a trusted friend, mentor, family member, or pastor to discuss your unique God-given gifts and how you might use your gifts to honor and glorify God. When you open your heart to God's purpose for you, God will fill your heart with the light of divine love, and that light will brighten every room you enter and enhance every relationship you have.

. . . when our predominant attitude is gratitude

**"Enter [the Lord's] gates with thanksgiving,
and his courts with praise! Give thanks to him,
bless his name!"**

Psalm 100:4 NRSV

Last spring, prior to my cancer diagnosis, I visited the cemetery on the outskirts of Magnolia, Arkansas, where my parents are buried. I placed on their headstone two red roses, which was my mom's favorite flower and the flower that my dad loved to bring home to her as a gift of love. I stood in silence beside the headstone for quite some time. Then I began to give thanks to God for the values that my parents taught me over the years through both their words and actions. One of their teachings was that adopting an attitude of gratitude was a choice and privilege offered to us by God. Their words and actions clearly indicated that they chose to live grateful lives, which brought great joy to them and their family.

Every meal in our home, regardless of whether our family was facing good times or encountering challenging times, began with Dad bowing his head and offering a prayer of thanksgiving for all the blessings the Lord had bestowed upon us, including the meal we were about to eat. I remember when Mom was in the middle of battling terminal colon cancer, she invited me to sit by her bed. She proceeded to let me know how thankful she was that she had been able to fulfill her God-given purpose to be a parent to my two sisters and me.

During occupational therapy this week, the therapist was working to bring down the swelling in my feet, legs, and left arm. I figured I must be quite a sight to my friends and family. I thought that I could easily be renamed "The Hulk" just in time for Halloween. However, before I knew it, I was giving God thanks that I had no swelling in my right hand and arm, the hand with which I write and the arm with which I greet my family and friends. A smile of joy spread across my face as I realized that my parents were the ones who had taught me to choose gratitude for the blessings God has given me over whining about what I don't have. Then I offered up thanks to God for my parents' positive influence on my life.

That day in the cemetery, before I walked back to my car, I looked up from my parents' headstone to see the depiction of the Lord's Supper on a monument just a few feet away. Knowing that in a few hours he would be arrested, tortured, and crucified on a cross, Jesus chose to give thanks by serving the Passover meal to his disciples. The bread and drink were symbols of the choice of a loving God to free his people from slavery and bondage. Soon, Jesus himself would be the divine symbol of freedom from the fear of sin and death; we are offered the choice of partaking in the sacrament of Holy Communion in observance of our redemption through Christ Jesus. My parents said yes to this choice to live a grateful life of faith. What do you choose?

. . . when we choose to **shine** rather than **whine**

> **"You are the light of the world. . . . let your light shine before others, so that they may see your good works and give glory to your Father in heaven."**
>
> Matthew 5:14-16 ESV

When life gets tough, we are all tempted to fall into the whining rut. The problem with succumbing to this temptation is that the rut continues to get deeper the longer we whine. Then, ultimately, we drive away the people who care about us because the energy drain on their emotions becomes intolerable. Our self-absorption (whining) communicates to our friends, who are ready and willing to help, that we either do not need them or do not value their friendship.

Over the years, a simple story from the post-WWII era has helped me climb out of the whining rut. After the war, a teenage boy responded to the loss of family and friends by creating a peace institute, where he eventually became an instructor. People from all over the world came to hear his engaging lectures. One day, at the end of his last class of the term, a tongue-in-cheek question came his way. With a wry smile, a student asked, "What is the meaning of life?"

The lecturer paused for a moment. Then he reached into his back pocket to retrieve his wallet. He pulled out a small, round mirror and said: "I found this piece of glass at the site of a motorcycle wreck during the war. The motorcycle belonged to a German soldier who had lost his life. Something led me to pick up this piece of shattered glass from the motorcycle's mirror. I fiddled with it for a while until I decided to polish its rough edges and place it in my wallet. During breaks from work or on weekends, I would remove the mirror from my wallet and reflect the light from the sun into dark corners of my home or dark crevices in the rocks. One day, my eyes and heart were opened to my purpose in life. I was meant to spend my days reflecting the light of peace and unconditional love into the darkness around us created by hate and greed. That is the purpose of my life. What is the purpose of yours?"

As followers of Christ, we are to be "the light of the world." Furthermore, we have been called upon by Christ himself to let Christ's light of peace and unconditional love shine before others so they can see our just and good works and give glory to our God in heaven. That is the purpose of a grace-filled, faithful life according to God's Word. What is the purpose of your life?

. . . when we choose Christlike **sacrifice** over selfish **ambition**

> **"Greater love has no one than this:**
> **to lay down one's life for one's friends."**
>
> John 15:13 NIV

A youth group program at First United Methodist Church, Van Buren, Arkansas began with a short film. "The Transformational Power of Unconditional Love" was announced by the youth pastor as the topic of our lesson. Based on a true story, the film opened with a German patrol entering a French village during World War II, looking for fighters with the French Resistance. The following is how I remember this film that I watched some fifty-eight years ago:

> Not one villager answered the inquiries from the German command. Therefore, the German captain lined up the villagers, including men, women, and children, against a row of haystacks. Then he assembled a firing squad to execute the entire village unless they revealed the whereabouts of the Resistance.
>
> After receiving no information, the captain ordered the firing squad to ready their rifles and aim. One man selected for the firing squad did not raise his rifle. The captain yelled, "Schultz, ready and

aim!" Schultz did not respond. The captain then shouted, "Schultz, either you ready your weapon to fire or join the villagers at the haystacks." Corporal Schultz placed his rifle on the ground in front of him. Then he took off his dog tags and put them on top of the gun. He did not take off the cross he was wearing around his neck. Schultz walked over to the haystack, turned to face the firing squad, and took the person's hand on his right and left. The film ended with smoke rising from the rifles of the firing squad at the site of a small village somewhere in France during World War II.

Over the years, I have asked myself whether Schultz had to die to reveal the love of Christ at work in that moment. What if he had just intentionally missed shooting any villager upon the order to fire? Over time, I have decided that intentionally missing would have communicated a kind of silent consent to the captain and his fellow officers that what they were doing that day was somehow all right. Schultz was not going to travel that course as a person of faith. Instead, he took the path followed by Jesus Christ himself, who showed his unconditional love by giving his life for us.

Since the needs of all of God's children are our top priority as followers of Jesus Christ, what are we willing to sacrifice to meet those needs? If not our physical life, what will we be willing to risk in order to build God's Kingdom of Love on earth as it is in heaven?

. . . when we give thanks for God's many blessings

> "Enter God's gates with thanksgiving,
> and his courts with praise!
> Give thanks to him; bless his name!
> For the LORD is good;
> his steadfast love endures forever,
> and his faithfulness to all generations."
>
> Psalm 100:4-5 NRSV

After spending an incredibly wonderful, long weekend with my Virginia granddaughters, Emogene (age five about to turn six), Joy (age two and a half), and their parents, Will and Amanda, I am now back home refreshed and filled with God's spirit of joy. However, upon my return, I had a somewhat troubling, reflective moment. I discovered a complaint deep down in my soul that bothered me. My experience with my two-and-a-half-year-old granddaughter was not the same experience I had with her during the first one-plus years of her life. I found that she was now far more independent and opinionated. Joy would sometimes say no when I would ask to hold her hand or ask her to give her Papaw a hug. My ideas about what we could play next were often soundly rejected for an entirely different plan in which I might or might not be included.

I found myself constantly dwelling on these troublesome developments until I remembered my boys' behavior in their early years. They went through something that we called "the terrible twos." However, this realization did not seem to fully diminish my sadness that maybe I had lost something in my relationship with my young granddaughter.

Blessedly, I had a moment that reminded me that Joy and I still maintain a special bond during these changing times. Joy consistently brought me books to read to her as she had done the last time that we were together. She not only handed me the book, but she planted herself in my lap, holding my hand or rubbing my now very bald head (chemotherapy-related). After reading more books to her in one sitting than I ever remembered reading to her before, she then indicated that it was her turn and proceeded to read several books to me. The smile of joy on her face was one that I will always cherish.

For most of us, the complaint department's door is always open, waiting for us to enter. However, we can choose to take the psalmist's advice instead. Let's walk through God's gate with a spirit of thanksgiving and into God's courtyard with praise for all the blessings in our lives.

This season, what complaint are you going to leave behind in order to enter God's thanksgiving gate? Joy is waiting for us in God's courtyard!

. . . when we have spiritual giants like Charles Stokes in our lives

> "A giant nearly ten feet tall stepped out from the Philistine line into the open: the champion Goliath from Gath. He was dressed in armor—126 pounds of it! Goliath stood there and called out to the Israelites, 'Pick your best fighter and pit him against me!'
>
> David the shepherd said, 'King Saul, don't give up hope. I am ready to go and fight this Philistine. God, who delivered me from the teeth of the lion and the claws of the bear, will deliver me from this Philistine.'"
>
> 1 Samuel 17:4-11, 32-37

Over the centuries, this Old Testament passage has been identified as the battle between David and a giant. However, the real giant in this story is not the physically gigantic Goliath, but the inexperienced youth named David. David was a spiritual giant because of the depth of his faith in God. Through David's faith, God's grace at work empowered him to overcome fear and certain defeat to face and subdue Goliath.

During a tough stretch of my battle with aggressive cancer, I picked up my cell phone and called my spiritual giant, Reverend Charles Stokes, to join me for lunch. Charles' strong faith and compassionate presence diminished my fear and significantly reduced the power I was allowing my diagnosis to have over me. Charles's words and presence gave me hope.

This was not the first time Charles had been an amazing pastor and friend to me and the St. Andrew family. When I approached Charles to become executive pastor of St. Andrew in 1987, he was already leading a phenomenal ministry at Highland Park United Methodist Church. Yet, Charles felt called to leave that work behind (and the job security it provided) to help a young, inexperienced pastor and a small growing faith fellowship become the church God created us to be. Charles' calm, kind, faithful, spirit, and his God-given gifts in the areas of worship, music, education, and finance led us through the birth pains of those four-and-a-half years in the school and into our first building.

At every turn, when there seemed to be a giant standing between us leaving the school to worship in our first facility, Charles challenged all of us to leave behind our fears and embrace the power of faith. I will never forget my nervousness on the day that St. Andrew was to have our first worship service in the new facility. The prior Sunday, Charles had organized a beautiful procession from the school where we had been worshiping to the new building. We carried the altar cross, Bible, communion chalice and plate, vestments, and banners from Shepton

High School to the new worship center. However, a major problem developed just before our first Sunday worship service in our new home. At midnight Saturday, the chairs and chancel furniture had not yet arrived. I drove to the church to find Charles (who was always steadfast in his belief that God was watching over us) waiting at the front door of our new worship center, confident that the furniture would come. It did arrive around 1:00 a.m. Then, he and the volunteers he had recruited worked until 2:30 a.m. to arrange the furniture so we could worship at 9:30 a.m. that very same morning. By the grace of God and with Charles' giant faith and leadership, we had faced another giant and subdued it.

I cannot count the hundreds of times over the last thirty-five years that Charles has served as my spiritual giant. He has provided love, support, joy, hope, and encouragement to me and my family. Furthermore, Charles has been the hands and feet of Christ to thousands of families and individuals who have made St. Andrew their spiritual home, empowering all of us to embrace faith over fear and hope over despair.

Charles Stokes had a heart attack and now resides in God's eternal heavenly kingdom, embraced by the unconditional love and abiding peace of our Lord and Savior, Jesus Christ. Though Charles is no longer physically with us, his giant faith and loving spirit will live on through the words and work of the St. Andrew family whom he so dearly loved and selflessly served. We love you, Charles!

. . . when we embrace God's gift of teamwork

"And behold, I am with you always, to the end of the age."

Matthew 28:20 ESV

At our family Thanksgiving gathering, my five-year-old granddaughter came to me and asked if this was my last Thanksgiving. She is aware that I am battling cancer, and I answered her as honestly as I possibly could. I told her I did not know for sure. This might be my last, or I might have more. However, what I do know is that this Thanksgiving was very special to me with her here, and I will cherish it always.

First, Thanksgiving was special because all my children and their families were present for our gathering. In addition, after our sumptuous meal, I was joyfully surprised by the presentation of special athletic wear before our annual sporting event. This year we played whiffle ball. My daughter-in-law, Amanda, gave each of us a bright red T-shirt sporting *Team Hasley* on the front along with a charging Razorback. Then, on the back of our T-shirts was our number and our name. My number was *01* and my name was *Papaw*. This athletic wear was unusual in that we did not wear different colored jerseys indicating two teams. We wore one color, identifying one team. We had only one logo, not multiple logos. We were all on the same team, from my eleven-month-old granddaughter to my forty-two-year-old eldest son. At the end of the game, I was presented an MVP trophy with love by my entire family affectionately known as *Team Hasley.*

Team Hasley, in fact, had been at work prior to Thanksgiving. The team began its work back in May when I was first diagnosed with aggressive cancer. Calls, texts, and invitations to visit from family members came my way.

With the help of her mom, my five-year-old granddaughter began sending me weekly videos entitled "Hall of Fame Baseball Jokes with Emogene" and my two-year-old granddaughter began sending videos to me entitled "Songs with Joy." Then, there were the many trips my family made to Plano, where hugs were shared, and family stories were told over and over again. Team Hasley made sure I knew that I was not facing this battle with cancer alone.

From the beginning, my family has been echoing the words of Christ: "I am with you always." My team has brought me strength, hope, and comfort. I know that, no matter what the future brings, I will not face it alone. Who is your team? If you don't have one, it is not too late to embrace one. If you already have a team, thank the Lord for them and hold them close.

. . . when we embrace the story
of Christmas

"For unto you is born this day in the city of David
a Savior, who is Christ the Lord."

Luke 2:11 ESV

The Lord God Almighty created us and placed us on this
earth for two purposes: to love God and love our neighbor. Joy comes to us as we strive to fulfill these purposes. Sin or separation is the result of turning our backs on
God and our neighbor for our own selfish ends. Often, our
children can help us to find our way back to whom God
created us to be.

I recall a couple in our church who told me they knew
early on that their child would one day choose a pub-
lic-service profession. I asked them how they might have
known this about their daughter at such an early age. They
told me this story:

Just before Christmas, Mom had taken her daughter
to a department store to buy her a warm jacket for the cold
winter weather. They found the perfect coat. The young
girl was wearing her new toasty garment as Mom paid the
cashier. When Mom finished paying, she turned around to
witness an event that she has cherished in her heart ever
since. Her daughter was walking out the front door of the

store alongside a mother and her daughter, who noticeably was wearing a summer dress on a very cold winter's day. Mom watched her daughter tap the girl on the shoulder. They both stopped just outside the sliding glass door. Then, her daughter proceeded to take off that new, perfectly fitting coat and hand it to the shivering girl. Her daughter then turned around, walked back into the store, and told her mom that this girl needed the coat more than she did.

May the Christ Child enter your heart this Christmas and lead you back to the joy of being all God created you to be.

. . . when we remember it is not **where** we go, but **who** we travel with

---

"Behold, the virgin shall conceive and bear a son,
and they shall call his name Immanuel"
(which means, God with us).

Matthew 1:23 ESV

My friend and brother in Christ, Reverend Charles Stokes, gave me a "Peanuts" comic strip a few years back captioned, "In life, it is not where you go, but whom you travel with." My friend's life exemplified this truth, as Charles faithfully and selflessly invested in relationships throughout his lifetime. The number one relationship in which he invested was his relationship with God. Second, he invested in his relationship with his family and with his neighbors. The love, joy, and hope that Charles experienced in his relationship with God overflowed into all his other relationships, which brought a smile to the face of all who knew him.

My prayer this Christmas is that, like Charles, we will all take time to invest in our relationship with God as revealed in the Christ Child. May we take a moment on Christmas Day to pause to remember that God so loved us that he gave to us his only Son, so that whoever chooses to believe in him (and invest in a relationship with him) will not perish but will know that God will be with us now and for eternity. The good news that Christ was born to us, with all our flaws and frailties, fills our hearts with unconditional love, joy, and hope that subsequently overflow into all our other relationships. This spiritual truth is why we believe that peace on earth is not only possible, but that God's peace will prevail. God is with us. Therefore, we can be confident that all who embrace the good news of Christ's birth will never be alone in this life or in the life to come. Thanks be to God for smiles!

... when we place our **trust** in the **Lord**

"For I know the plans I have for you, declares the LORD, plans for good and not for evil, to give you a future with hope."

Jeremiah 29:11

In the past, I would begin each new year with a list of new-year resolutions. My success at keeping those resolutions was always mixed at best. Then I came across a covenant prayer attributed to John Wesley. Since that moment, I have chosen to pray this covenant prayer rather than craft a list of personal resolutions for each new year. I have found that placing my complete trust in the Lord God Almighty has brought me the gift of divine hope in a way that my self-crafted resolutions could not. This year, 2022, is no exception, as I face an uphill battle with aggressive cancer. I pray that the following covenant prayer will serve as a divine hope-filled gift for you, as it has for me.

"A Covenant Prayer in the Wesleyan Tradition"

I am no longer my own, but yours.
Put me to what you will, rank me with whom
you will.
Put me to doing, put me to suffering.
Let me be employed by you or laid aside by you,

exalted for you or brought low by you.
Let me be full, let me be empty.
Let me have all things, let me have nothing.
I freely and heartily yield all things to your pleasure and disposal.
And now, O glorious and blessed God, Father,
Son, and Holy Spirit, you are mine, and I am yours.
So be it.
And the covenant which I have made on earth,
let it be ratified in heaven.
Amen.[3]

[3] Adapted from "A Covenant Prayer in the Wesleyan Tradition," The United Methodist Hymnal (Nashville: The United Methodist Publishing House, 1989), 607.

. . . when we know God stands on both sides of the grave

"For I am sure that neither death nor life . . . nor height nor depth, nor anything else in all creation, will be able to separate us from the love of God in Christ Jesus our Lord."

Romans 8:38-39 ESV

While walking down the hallway of a nearby hospital, I spotted the church member I had come to visit. He was leaning up against the wall outside of his wife's hospital room. She had been diagnosed with terminal cancer.

With tears in his eyes, he looked up at me and said, "I do not know how anyone goes through something as heartbreaking as this without having God in their lives."

At that moment, the truth of Tom's words touched my heart and mind in a way that I never thought possible. My good friend and sidekick in ministry for over twenty-six years, Reverend Charles Stokes, expanded upon Tom's affirmation of faith when he offered these comforting words at a memorial service: "Hold tightly to the reality that God stands on both sides of the grave."

Both Tom and Charles joined the Apostle Paul in declaring that only through faith in God through Jesus

Christ do we find a hope that never dies. Only in knowing that nothing can ever separate us from the love of God in Christ Jesus are we able to continue to put one foot in front of the other in difficult circumstances. Our faith gives us incredible strength to face life's challenges because we believe that we will never face anything, even death itself, alone.

. . . when we **give thanks**
for our **blessings**

"Make a joyful noise to the LORD, all the earth.
. . . Enter his gates with thanksgiving, and his courts
with praise. Give thanks to him; bless his name.
For the LORD is good; his steadfast love endures
forever, and his faithfulness to all generations."

Psalm 100:1, 4-5 NRSV

My seventieth birthday has prompted me to pause to reflect upon my journey over these years. I've experienced
extremely difficult seasons, during which the losses of ones
I loved and admired brought profound heartbreak and
personal struggle. Then there were the celebratory years
of births, baptisms, weddings, and personal and profes-
sional success that have brought great joy and fulfillment
to my life. However, what I have come to believe over time
is that difficult years and celebratory years are not mutu-
ally exclusive when it comes to blessings bestowed. Often,
during those most challenging years, I have felt tremendous gratitude that the Lord is good, and that God's love
and faithfulness endures forever.

During my mom's tenacious battle with colon cancer,
I remember giving thanks for the overwhelming love and

support of our faith family. The youth group from First United Methodist Church of Magnolia, Arkansas, showed up unannounced with rakes in their hands. They raked the fallen leaves in our yard, bagged them, and carried them away. The pastor of our local Wesley Foundation knew of my mom's bucket list, which included riding a motorcycle one day. The pastor showed up at our house riding a Harley. My mom and Reverend Arnold proceeded to cruise the streets of Magnolia on that Harley, which not only brought great joy to Mom but gave the town something to smile and talk about for months to come. After Mom's passing into the Lord's eternal embrace, I returned to Plano and St. Andrew to lead Sunday worship and communion. I cannot tell you how many people took my hand while I served communion. They let me know that day that they had been praying for my mom and me. The light of God's love truly shined through our beloved family of faith during the darkness of those days. For the strength and hope that our faith family gave to the Hasley family, I will forever give thanks.

. . . because of the power of the cross

"For the word of the cross is folly to some, but to those who are being saved it is the power of God."

1 Corinthians 1:18

After washing up, putting on my pajamas, and hitting the pillow, I paused last night to reflect on my navigation of months of cancer treatments. Needless to say, it has not been all smooth sailing during my battle to slow down aggressive cancer. Yet, after nine months, I am stronger and more active than I ever imagined I would be. "Why?" I asked as I looked upward for an answer. By God's grace, I came to understand the power of the cross at work in my life more clearly.

When I placed my head on my pillow, I instinctively reached out with my right hand to hold hands with my wife. I realized that I could not have traveled this far with my diagnosis without her love, prayers, and support, along with the support of my immediate family, my faith family, and my friends. With my left hand, I reached out to check the flow of the pump filled with chemicals to slow down the cancer growth. What a blessing, I pondered, that the Lord God Almighty has called upon so many selfless doctors, nurses, technicians, hospital staff, and medical researchers to improve and save lives.

As my arms stretched out east and west, my legs extended south over a pillow that I had placed at the foot of my bed. According to the instructions of my occupational therapist, elevating my feet, ankles, and legs helps to prevent fluid buildup. It is working. I can now more easily place one foot in front of the other each day as I fulfill my desire to continue to be the feet and hands of Christ as a pastor at St. Andrew.

My revelation last night was that my reclining body was positioned in the shape of a cross. My arms were stretched horizontally to connect with my wife and my medical team's solution to slowing down my cancer. My legs and head represented the cross's vertical dimension, ultimately pointing to God's heavenly kingdom. My thoughts turned to the power of God's unconditional grace and sacrificial love revealed by the cross. We can find great power in the cross if we believe and tap into that power. When the power of the cross dwells in our heart, mind, and soul, nothing (not cancer, treatments, or even death itself) can separate us from God's love and hope.

... when we embrace the **divine power** of our **index finger**

**"Let no one seek their own good,
but the good of their neighbor."**

1 Corinthians 10:24 ESV

My thirteen-and-a-half-month-old granddaughter, Aashni, has recently discovered the power in her index finger. For example, a week ago my son John and I took Aashni to the Fort Worth Zoo. Our itinerary that day was set by Aashni and her index finger. All she had to do was point, and that was the direction we headed. She pointed to the giraffe, and we proceeded to walk over to where the giraffe was feeding in his enclosure. Aashni pointed to the elephant. We moved to the place where we had the best view of the baby elephant, Brazos, who was hanging out with his mom, Bluebonnet. She pointed to the river otters swimming in a water tank. We stopped to watch them swim on their backs underwater while leaving a stream of air bubbles in their wake. Then she pointed toward the sound coming from the bird sanctuary. We stopped in front of the habitat of the African Fish Eagle as it loudly screeched its rather strong feelings to those of us gathered there. Aashni's index finger created connections that brought smiles to our faces and joy to our hearts.

I remember an iconic painting on the ceiling in the Sistine Chapel by Michelangelo where God's index finger is extended to create and connect with the first human being. I believe that this index finger moment brought joy to God's heart and a smile to his face. I believe that each time we, in the image of God, create connections with God's creation and one another, God smiles upon us with a joyful heart. However, sometimes extending an index finger toward someone is not intended to create and connect but instead to destroy and disconnect. I think of the fingers of religious leaders, as recorded in the New Testament, pointed toward a woman accused of adultery with rocks for stoning held in their other hands. I think of the crowd pointing to Jesus as they shouted to Pilate, "Crucify him!" In each case, God stepped in to point a finger toward the religious leaders and the crowd. Jesus extended his finger on behalf of God the Father not to destroy or to disconnect, but to create a new heart and spirit with words like, "You who are without sin cast the first stone" (John 8:7) and "Father, forgive them for they know not what they do" (Luke 23:34 ESV). God is love, as revealed by the use of God's index finger to create and connect.

My granddaughter Aashni uses her index finger in another way that I have not yet mentioned. She points to her mom and dad with the expectation they will point back to her, touching their index finger to hers. Aashni has just begun doing the same with me, her Papaw. Let me tell you, each time we touch the ends of our index fingers, a huge smile comes to my face, and my heart is transformed into pure joy. Maybe we all could increase the use of our index fingers to communicate unconditional love. I can personally testify that the outcome is divine joy.

... because we have got this

"For all things are possible with God."

Mark 10:27 ESV

Today, I looked down at the wrist bracelet that I had received from a very good friend immediately following my cancer diagnosis. I have worn it now on my right wrist for over nine months. Printed on the bracelet are the words, "You Got This." I greatly appreciated the positive approach to my diagnosis back then, but frankly, it has taken me until now to grasp what it really means to believe "I Got This." It does not mean I will be cured, but it also does not mean that by God's miraculous grace I will not somehow be cured, either. It does not mean the chemo treatments will be smooth sailing. It does not mean I will not have moments that I am afraid and anxious about what the future holds.

However, what "You Got This" has come to mean to me is that I am not alone in my battle with cancer. The fact that my family, friends, and church family have chosen to walk alongside me during this challenging time means the world to me. I would not have had the strength to travel this path without them or the strong presence of Christ in my life. Recently, I received a text from one of my friends who has chosen to walk this road with me. My friend reminded me that I have a choice. I can either wake up each day choosing to "live with cancer," or I can choose to spend my day "dying with cancer." You (my loving family and friends) and the good Lord above remind me each day that "I Got This." Because of your encouragement and compassion, I am choosing to "live with cancer." This choice has brought me a level of purpose, joy, hope, and fulfillment that I would have never thought possible under the circumstances.

Therefore, I leave you with this thought. No matter how rocky the road is you are traveling today, know "You Got This!"

. . . when we embrace God's miracles

> "God also testified to it by signs, wonders, and various miracles, and by gifts of the Holy Spirit distributed according to his will."
>
> Hebrews 2:4 NIV

The day I was diagnosed with aggressive cancer, I did not place that unwelcome news in the miracle category. Today, however, ten months after that diagnosis, I see God's hand at work regarding the timing of the diagnosis. I had just returned from a fishing trip with friends when I felt a sharp pain in my abdomen. My initial thought was that I had a kidney stone or a gallstone. I asked my daughter to drive me to the emergency room to get relief from the pain and to confirm my self-diagnosis. The pain subsided, but I was wrong about the diagnosis. Stage four pancreatic cancer was the verdict.

I was devastated by the totally unexpected news. However, over time, I have grown to be thankful for catching the disease far earlier than I might have. According to the doctor, the abdominal pain was very uncommon considering the location of the cancer cells. Typically, I would not have experienced symptoms for months to come. However, because I experienced the pain (which I have not experienced since), I was able to immediately start chemo treatments to slow down the rapid cancer growth.

The miracle of the early diagnosis is that I have experienced ten months of cancer treatments, which have slowed down cancer growth and allowed me to stay active. I have spent significant quality time with family and friends, bringing me great joy. I continue to serve as a pastor to the St. Andrew family I cherish. I have traveled with family and friends to several "bucket list" locations, which has been a true blessing.

Therefore, I count it a miracle that I was able to spend Valentine's weekend with three of my granddaughters. I watched my six-year-old granddaughter, Emogene, climb up a ladder to reach the rings spaced out at a height above the ground that required a child to swing from ring to ring, one by one, to reach the ladder at the opposite end. As she made her way from one end of the rings to the other, she fell. Then, she fell again and again, which I thought would have ended her mission. However, with determination and persistence, along with an occasional hug from her Papaw, she kept getting back up and starting again until she made it from one end of the rings to the other without falling. The miracle was that Emogene never gave up, even when it seemed she was facing an impossible task.

You know, just when you think your role as a grandparent is to teach your grandchild how to navigate the challenges of life, they can (and do) end up teaching you. Jesus reminds us that "to our children belongs the kingdom of God" (Mark 10:14). Emogene taught me a kingdom principle that day. When you fall, God has given us the power of his grace and love of family to provide a shining example or an encouraging hug to help us get back up and keep going. God's grace and the love of family are miracles that give us strength in our time of need. God is good!

... when we carry a song in our hearts

"Make a joyful noise to the LORD, all the earth!
Serve the LORD with gladness!
Come into his presence with singing."

Psalm 100:1-2 ESV

My son Will brought his wife, Amanda, and two of their daughters, Emogene and Joy, to Plano from Virginia to visit Sharon and me for Valentine's Day weekend. On Saturday, we loaded into the car to travel to the Dallas Arboretum to meet up with my son John and his family for a relaxing afternoon. My three-year-old granddaughter, Joy, made our outing memorable.

Adjacent to where we set up our picnic was a small rock bridge extending over a tiny moat to a small island with a single tree located in the center. I followed Joy as she crossed over the moat onto the island. She then pointed toward the tree to let me know that the tree was now a castle. Then she proceeded to break out into song (a song I recognized from the motion picture *Frozen*) and to dance. The sparkle in her eyes and the smile on her face projected the pure joy that was in her heart.

Joy is not a word I would use to characterize my chemo treatment experience. However, I took a page out of Joy's Dallas Arboretum agenda and carried my iPhone to the cancer center for my chemo treatment. Like Joy, I used my imagination to transport myself to a different place than a hospital room. I imagined that I was in an enchanted forest with majestic south Arkansas pine trees and radiant fall-colored hardwood surrounding me. Then I tapped my Spotify app and was immediately immersed in a beautiful world of music. As cancer-fighting chemicals filled my body, I sang "Unchained Melody" and "Amazing Grace" while *dancing* in the enchanted forest. Joy filled my soul that day amid what is normally an anxiety-filled chemo treatment.

God's gift of song has a way of lifting our spirits, as it did for the psalmist, for Joy, and now for me. Therefore, maybe it is time for us to sing and dance more. For in our singing and dancing, the Lord God Almighty knows that we can find great joy!

. . . because God shepherds us through storms with uplifting memories

"And when they got into the boat, the wind ceased.
And those in the boat worshiped him saying,
'Truly you are the Son of God.'"

Matthew 14:32-33 ESV

On the afternoon of Friday, November 22, 1963, my sixth-grade teacher, Mrs. Wallace, entered our classroom with tears in her eyes. She announced that the thirty-fifth president of the United States, John F. Kennedy, had been shot. Tears welled up in the eyes of us all upon hearing this heartbreaking news. I still remember the peace and comfort that Mrs. Wallace provided for us with a prayer and with her presence. She reminded us that God was watching over the Kennedy family, our nation, and our sixth-grade class, and that she was there for us, as well.

When I heard the news that Russia was waging war with Ukraine, my heart broke as I envisioned the thousands of lives that would be lost in such an invasion, including innocent adults, youth, and children. I immediately wanted to do something to help those caught in the middle of this deadly storm but ultimately felt an overwhelming sense of helplessness. Then, I remembered how my teacher, Mrs. Wallace, handled the storm back in 1963. On that day, she reminded us with a prayer that God loves us and would watch over us through this troubling time. She then added that she was present for us to offer a listening ear, comforting words, and hugs.

This God-given memory has served to help me navigate my response to the Ukrainian crisis. I have prayed that the Lord God Almighty will watch over the people in harm's way, especially the innocent children and youth, and soften hardened hearts to end this war immediately.

Furthermore, during these last few days, I have consciously made an effort to be a better listener, speak more comforting words, and offer more signs of compassion. Thank you, Mrs. Wallace, for your steadfast faith that allowed God's grace to work in and through you to provide guidance, strength, and comfort amid a terrible storm. May we stand firm in our faith and actions like Mrs. Wallace as, together, we encounter another heartbreaking moment that is facing our brothers and sisters in Ukraine.

. . . when love is in the air

"Anyone who does not love does not know God, because God is love."

1 John 4:8 ESV

A very dear friend made it possible for my three sons, Stephen, John, and Will, and me to spend a few days vacationing in Scottsdale, Arizona. We played golf and did some sightseeing, but one of the most unforgettable moments was observing the courtship of a male and female Anna's Hummingbird. In the backyard of the home where we stayed, the female was perched in a tree, making an unusual chirping sound. Then we spotted the male Anna's Hummingbird high up in the sky directly above us. He performed an aerial display for the female, rising high in the sky (130 feet or more) and then diving back down toward her. At the bottom of the dive, the male produced an audible sound caused by the tail feathers, best described as an explosive squeak. He also boasted an iridescent reddish-pink crown, which served to grab the attention of the female. Love was definitely in the air at that special moment.

That remarkable event opened my eyes to the love happening all around me. In the butterfly exhibit we visited, I saw a mom bend down to show her young son how to coax a butterfly to land on his index finger. Love was in the air. At a cactus garden exhibit, a husband and wife were walking down the trail hand in hand, lovingly looking at each other every few steps. Love was in the air. During my golf game with my three sons, I frequently reflected upon how special this time was that we had together, especially amid my battle with cancer. I pondered how much I love them and how proud I am of each one of them. Love was in the air.

Reflecting upon our spiritual life, love was in the air as Jesus healed the sick, fed thousands with a few fish and loaves of bread, and gave his life on a cross so that we might be free from fear to live with the hope and joy of faith. Christ's love is still in the air today. I pray that you will not only open your eyes and your heart to see God's love at work all around you, but that you will be a frequent purveyor of divine love to others.

. . . when you **believe** in **eternal life**

"For God so loved the world, that he gave his only Son,
that whoever believes in him should not perish
but have eternal life."

John 3:16 ESV

Over the years, I have witnessed the damage that the fear of death and dying can inflict upon us and our relationships. When fear takes hold of us, we often become paralyzed, and the quality of our life is greatly diminished.

However, if we choose to believe in the divine promise of eternal life, fear's grip over us is loosened. We are then free to experience the joy of actively pursuing our God-given purpose in this life: to love God and our neighbor with words and deeds.

A frequently asked question that I field as a pastor is "What is eternal life like?" or "What is heaven like?" I often struggle with the answer; the Bible does not elaborate on what we will experience in life after death. Therefore, what eternal life is like God has left primarily to our imaginations. I especially like the vision of dying culminating in eternal life, revealed in a famous poem widely attributed to Reverend Henry Van Dyke. My prayer is that this poem will reinforce your belief in eternal life.

"Gone From My Sight"

I am standing upon the seashore.

A ship, at my side, spreads her white sails to the moving breeze and starts for the blue ocean.

She is an object of beauty and strength, and I stand and watch her until, at length, she hangs like a speck of white cloud just where the sea and sky come to mingle with each other.

Then someone at my side says, "There, she is gone."

Gone where? Gone from my sight. That is all.

She is just as large in mast, hull and spar as she was when she left my side, and, she is just as able to bear her load of living freight to the destined port.

Her diminished size is in me—not in her.

And, just at the moment when someone says, "There, she is gone," there are other eyes watching her coming, and other voices ready to take up the glad shout, "Here she comes!"

And that is—"dying."[4]

· ·

[4] Adapted from the poem that appears in Barbara Karnes RN, *Gone from My Sight: The Dying Experience* (Barbara Karnes Publishing, 2008), https://bkbooks.com/

... because God's grace helps us navigate life's storms

"And a great windstorm arose, and the waves were breaking into the boat, so that the boat was already filling . . . And [Jesus] awoke and rebuked the wind and said to the sea, 'Peace! Be still!' And the wind ceased and there was great calm."

Mark 4:37-39 ESV

As a way to navigate the storm of cancer that is swirling inside me, I took a bucket-list trip to New York with my three sons last weekend. We visited my best friend from high school, Aubrey, who shared tall tales about our heroic football and baseball exploits back in the day. Then my boys and I traveled to Cooperstown, where we toured the National Baseball Hall of Fame with its many exhibits of boyhood heroes such as Willie Mays and Mickey Mantle. We concluded the trip with a visit to the national 9/11 Memorial at the World Trade Center, which honors the fallen and the first responders on that tragic day. We left the 9/11 Memorial with a heavy heart as we reflected upon the thousands of innocent lives lost; however, we were also inspired by the bravery of the rescuers who risked their lives to save the lives of others from a storm of fire, smoke, and falling debris.

All of us encounter storms throughout our life, whether they consist of an unwanted medical diagnosis, a catastrophic loss of loved ones, or a drastic change in fortunes. At those moments, we yearn for someone to guide us through the storm to a place of peace and calm. Over the years, I have come to believe that God sends rescuers (some might call them Christ-like angels) to help us navigate the storms that threaten us. I'm positive that angels stood on the stairs of the north and south towers of the World Trade Center, guiding people to safety during a deadly firestorm.

An angel by the name of Taylor Davis guided us, in the midst of our fear and concern over the lives lost in a vicious war in Ukraine, to the sanctuary of our church, where we could find peace and calm through inspirational music during this tragic storm. The evening culminated in an opportunity to give a love offering to those struggling to survive in Ukraine. God sent me an angel too, my wife Sharon, who has encouraged me to take these bucket-list trips with family and friends. The resulting calm and peace I have felt amid the storm of cancer I attribute to Sharon's unconditional love and support.

Who is the Christ-like angel you can count on during your stormy days? Better yet, for whom can you be an angel today?

. . . when our **focus** is upon
celebrating new life

"Therefore, be imitators of God, as beloved children. And walk in love, as Christ loved us and gave himself up for us, a fragrant offering and sacrifice to God."

Ephesians 5:1-2 ESV

Just as God celebrated his joyful creation of humankind from the dust of the earth, breathed life into us, and then called all that he created good, we are called upon to celebrate God's daily creations that bring joy to our souls.

This past month, I have noticed the bright red blooms of the redbud tree. Sitting for long stretches of time enjoying the redbud tree blooming just a few steps from our patio has been one of my favorite pastimes during March. Additionally, I drive to St. Andrew just to get a glimpse of the redbud trees majestically lining the creek and to behold those that are beautifully enveloping the Good Shepherd Columbarium. When I give myself permission to pause and focus upon the wonder of creation, all that is troublesome begins to fade into the background, with divine joy taking center stage.

Monday afternoon of this week, I received an amazing photo on my phone from my son John, of my won-

---

derful daughter-in-law Ananya, holding their "incredibly handsome" newborn baby boy. Pure joy radiated from her smile and from the sparkle in her eyes. Her joy was contagious as his Nana and Papaw (me) grinned ear to ear from daylight into the night until dawn the next day when we were both able to hold our grandson, Arin Carlton Hasley, for the first time. Immediately, we fell head-over-heels in love with him. Again, all our worries, concerns, and personal agendas took a back seat to our celebration of the remarkable joy of new life!

As we celebrate Palm Sunday, Holy Week, and Easter Sunday this year, may joy fill your heart and may a smile stretch from ear to ear across your face as we declare together, "Hallelujah, Christ Is Risen!" Then, may our joy in Christ Jesus spill over into our every word and action so that others may see in us the power of God's life-giving grace and desire divine grace for themselves.

. . . when we draw strength from our grace-filled past

> "I have fought the good fight, I have finished the race, I have kept the faith."
>
> 2 Timothy 4:7 ESV

As I approach the one-year mark of battling aggressive cancer, I celebrate the people who have served as instruments of God's grace to give me the strength to fight the good fight and keep the faith. I think of my mom, who waged war with colon cancer with a piece of notebook paper on her bedside table, upon which she had written her favorite, uplifting Scripture passages. Among her last words to me were, "I am at peace because I have accomplished what the Lord has placed me upon the earth to do. My greatest blessing was giving birth to you and your two sisters and watching you grow into the special people you are today." I remember too my 101-year-old grandmother, Maude Stephens, who, with her last breath, was still singing and playing on the nursing home piano the great and glorious hymns of the church. Then there was my father, whose joy for life was evident in his laughter that, until his final day with us, echoed throughout our home and the hallways of the public schools over which he was superintendent.

Their strength came from God's grace at work in their lives, made possible because of the divine gift of their deep and abiding faith in the risen Christ. The gift of God's grace through faith was passed down to them from their parents and grandparents, and that same faith they lovingly passed down to my sisters and me. I thank the Lord for placing my parents and grandparents in my life to show me the divine path of strength. They taught me that joy and purpose is a gift of God's grace that is meant to be received and then passed on to others. My heartfelt prayer is that I might pass on the gift of God's strength to my children, grandchildren, and neighbors like my parents and grandparents passed on to me.

. . . when we **ask** for **help** when needed

"Even though I walk through the valley of the shadow
of death, I will fear no evil, for you are with me;
your rod and your staff, they comfort me."

Psalm 23:4 ESV

As a pastor, shepherd, and provider of help to others over the past forty-six years, I have been filled with the joy of loving relationships and a lasting, meaningful purpose. However, I have not been as accomplished when asking for help when I have had a personal need. I do converse with the Lord about my struggles and challenges. The Lord himself asked for help when, for instance, he declared from the cross upon which he was crucified: "I thirst" (John 19:28 ESV). On the other hand, I have been more reticent when it comes to sharing my needs with family members and friends.

I know that my ongoing battle with this aggressive cancer has changed my heart and thinking when it comes to asking for help and assistance to effectively navigate this incredibly challenging time in my life. I find myself leaning on the strength of my wife Sharon, who has navigated her own health issues with grace and determination.

My sister Barbara has, for a year now, gone with me to hear the reports from my oncologist following CT scans.

She takes time away from her work to be with me to write down important information from my doctor that I might miss otherwise. Most important, she is there for me to hold onto when the news is not so positive, and I share it on the phone with my sister Sara in Louisiana. My three sons and daughter have wonderful ways of checking in on me and being there for me to make special memories, like dropping by our apartment to visit, sometimes with my granddog, Teddy, eating out together, or going to sporting events. They've also taken special trips with me to Virginia to see my granddaughters, to Denver to see my grandcat, and to Montana to see a future family home site. We've also visited Arizona for Major League Baseball spring training and golf; the 9/11 Memorial at the World Trade Center; the Baseball Hall of Fame in Cooperstown; to see my good friend in Bronxville, New York; and most recently, to Arkansas for a trip down memory lane.

My oldest son, Stephen, joined two of my good friends and me for a weekend in Hot Springs. Then Stephen took me by car on a six-day trip to memorable places in Arkansas. He made all the plans for places to stay, eat, and visit. He first drove me to Gum Springs and Gurdon, where my parents grew up, married, and had me baptized. Gurdon was where my Grandmother Stephens modeled for me the beauty and strength of a deep and abiding faith. Next, he drove me to First United Methodist Church in Magnolia and Magnolia High School, where I remembered my youth director, Billy Boyd Smith, and my football coach,

Don Hubbard. Both had a tremendous influence on my life. Billy Boyd taught me the meaning of Christ-like, selfless service. Coach Hubbard passed on to me the values of honesty, integrity, and an exemplary work ethic (as did both of my parents). They all helped me to become the person I am today. Motivated by unconditional love, they were there to support, encourage, and help me in times of need. They gave me something I never asked for, but they were there to help me anyway. What a powerful blessing for which I had done nothing to deserve, nonetheless, for which I am truly grateful and humbled. All the above I experienced on the first full day of my trip. I had five more days, joyful days just like them, because of the unconditional love and heartfelt, compassionate love of my son Stephen.

I returned to Plano with more hope and energy than I had felt in months. This trip was medicine for my heart and soul. Stephen helped me in ways I can never possibly express to him in words alone. The conversations and the stories we shared were a highlight of our time together. I felt closer to Stephen by opening my heart to his remarkable gift during my illness, just as I have grown closer to my wife, sisters, children, daughters-in-law, grandchildren, nieces, nephew, and friends because of their generous hearts. All that is required of me to connect with family and friends in amazing, wonderful ways is to say yes to their offers of help amidst my effort to navigate this unpredictable and insidious cancer I am battling. They have all helped me to focus on making each day count. For me, this means choosing to receive help and to help others each day the good Lord puts breath in my lungs. I am so very blessed because my loving helpers who surround me have taught me to focus on "living with cancer" and not "dying with cancer."

My prayer for you is that you embrace the balanced life that the risen Christ has in mind for you, which is a life spent receiving help from God and others during our times of need and serving as a helper when others are in need.

. . . when you spend your **life** on something that **outlasts** it

"For even the Son of Man came not to be served but to serve, and to give his life as a ransom for many."

Mark 10:45 ESV

I was sitting in the chemo recliner, watching my nurse expertly mix the chemicals I would be infused with to battle my cancer. As I have been known to do, I teased him a little, saying, "If you took your skill of mixing chemicals and used it to mix drinks at a local bar, my hunch is that you would make really good money with the tips that would come your way." My nurse paused for a second, looked straight at me, and replied, "I already receive great tips here at the cancer center. My tips consist of 'giving life' to cancer patients. It does not get better than this." As a one-year recipient of his expertise in giving life to those of us with illnesses that threaten to take away our lives, I have an accurate understanding of what he had just voiced. He feels his work is a calling from God Almighty, the benefits of which will far outlast his own life span.

If we stop to contemplate the meaning of Easter, we are reminded that Jesus himself spent his life on that which has endured. He used his life to serve the Lord God Almighty by giving his life on a cross so that we might be freed (ransomed) from the bondage of the fear of sin and death. Then Jesus stepped out of a tomb on Easter morning to prove to all who had eyes to see and ears to hear that believing in him meant joining Jesus in the gift of a life lived in faith, not fear; in hope, not despair; in love, not hate. Eternal life in the loving embrace of our Lord awaits us, at which time we will be reunited with the saints who have gone before us. What a glorious vision for all of us to celebrate and in which we can all find great comfort, assurance, and peace!

I pray that you might know eternal peace and lasting hope by placing your heart, soul, and mind in the hands of our crucified and risen Christ. By so doing, you will choose to spend your life on something that outlasts it.

. . . when **trusting** in **God's grace** we adjust to **overcome** life's **roadblocks**

**"Create in me a clean heart, O God,
and renew a right spirit within me."**

Psalm 51:10 ESV

I recently returned with a great group of friends from a trout fishing trip to the White River close to Cotter, Arkansas. Dave, our guide, asked Hank and me whether we wanted to fish for little trout, like the rainbow, or big trout, like the brown. Hank and I were quick to respond, "The big browns, of course." Now that was the easy part of our fishing adventure. Next, the guide took us to the most likely spots in the river to catch brown trout.

After trying several places, we were not getting bites, so Dave began making adjustments. He increased and then decreased the depth of the lure. He changed out the flies several times that we were using to hook the fish.

At the same time, he patiently coached Hank and me on our casting skills. Eventually, the adjustments worked, and Hank and I caught over twenty trout between us that day, including some nice-sized browns. All of this was possible because our guide was willing to adjust to the challenging conditions of the river, the fickle appetite of the trout, and our casting technique to have the best opportunity of landing a nice-sized trout.

Our Heavenly Guide modeled for us the importance of adjusting to roadblocks that life throws in our path. Jesus began his ministry with a clear calling, as recorded in the Gospel of Luke:

The Spirit of the Lord is upon me,
because he has anointed me
to proclaim good news to the poor.
He has sent me to proclaim liberty to the captives
and recovering of sight to the blind,
to set at liberty those who are oppressed,
to proclaim the year of the Lord's favor.
(Luke 4:18-19 ESV)

Yet the religious leaders did not hear or accept Jesus' authority or teaching, so he had to adapt to overcome the roadblocks. His adjustment led to a trial, a beating, and a cross, followed by the eternal hope of an empty tomb. Our joyous Easter celebration is an outgrowth of Jesus' life adjustment, made possible by the strength of his faith in his Heavenly Father's presence and divine grace at work in his life.

We all face roadblocks throughout our life journeys. My prayer for you today is that you embrace that our loving and merciful God has given to us, through faith, the gift to be able to adapt and overcome the challenges and burdens we face. If we open our minds and hearts to God's guiding presence each day, God will lead us on an incredible journey where we will overcome our fear, despair, and loneliness with faith, hope, and love. Like a successful fishing trip with an amazing guide, the result is a smile on our faces and joy in our hearts. Thanks be to God!

. . . when we **make** each day **count**

> "And every day, in the temple and from house to house,
> [the apostles] did not cease teaching and preaching
> that the Christ is Jesus."
>
> Acts 5:42 ESV

Over my forty-six years of ministry, I have made many a
pastoral visit to someone who has had a loved one unex-
pectedly pass on to God's heavenly kingdom; I have often sat by the bedside of someone who is taking their last
breath. My takeaway from those heart-rending moments
is that none of us knows how long we or our loved ones
will walk this earth before we are called to God's eternal
kingdom. Therefore, one of the primary questions that I
have been asked or I have asked myself when facing mortality is how I will choose to spend the time I have on
this earth. What will I do with my life until I take my last
breath?

In the middle of my battle with terminal cancer, a
prayer attributed to St. Francis of Assisi has provided me
an answer to how I can best make each day count. Pray the
St. Francis Prayer with me:

> Lord, make me an instrument of thy peace;
> where there is hatred, let me sow love;
> where there is injury, pardon;

where there is doubt, faith;
where there is despair, hope;
where there is darkness, light;
and where there is sadness, joy.
O Divine Master,
grant that I may not so much seek to be consoled
as to console;
to be understood, as to understand;
to be loved, as to love;
for it is in giving that we receive,
it is in pardoning that we are pardoned,
and it is in dying that we are born to eternal life.

When we are connecting with the Lord, our family, and neighbors, and when we are lovingly serving the Lord by loving and serving others, we are doing that which matters. For the next week, start your day by praying this prayer. Then, ask at the end of the week whether you took a step forward toward making each day count with the Lord's help.

... when by God's grace we can keep on keeping on

> ### "Who will sustain you to the end, guiltless in the day of our Lord Jesus Christ?"
>
> 1 Corinthians 1:8

Bishop Kenneth Pope's wife of over fifty years had died just a few weeks before I encountered him in the hallway of Perkins School of Theology at SMU. I shared with him that he had been in my prayers. Then I asked him how he was doing. "By the grace of God," he said, "I am putting one foot in front of the other." Amidst his tremendous grief, Bishop Pope's response has helped to sustain me in some of the most difficult moments in my life.

First, Bishop Pope was clear that he had chosen to lean on God's grace to navigate his devastating loss. He knew that he could not face the future alone. Therefore, he turned to the Lord to comfort and sustain him in his time of pain and sorrow. The Apostle Paul's reassuring words come to mind:

> Who shall separate us from the love of Christ? Shall tribulation, or distress, or persecution, or famine, or nakedness, or danger, or sword? . . . No, in all things we are more than conquerors through him

who loved us. For I am sure that neither death nor life, nor angels nor rulers, nor things present nor things to come, nor powers, nor height nor depth, nor anything else in all of creation, will be able to separate us from the love of God in Christ Jesus our Lord. (Romans 8:35, 37-39 ESV)

Second, Bishop Pope recognized his limitations during his season of mourning. His focus was not on accomplishing monumental tasks. Instead, he concentrated on just getting up in the morning and placing one foot in front of the other. During my one-year battle with cancer, I have been tempted to tackle impossible tasks. However, I encountered only frustration and disappointment in doing so. When I recognized my limitations and paced myself, however, I found fulfillment and joy as I moved toward achieving reasonable goals.

I thank the Lord for the witness of faithful servants like Bishop Pope, who have helped to shepherd me and others along life's winding road. I pray that you and I might honor him and those faithful guides who have gone before us by embracing the opportunity to shepherd others along narrow and difficult paths.

... when we **take** the **time** to do some **puddle stomping**

"Make a joyful noise unto the LORD, all the earth!"

Psalm 100:1 ESV

I took a trip this past weekend to Crozet, Virginia, to visit my grandchildren. Rain changed much of our anticipated joy-filled outdoor agenda. However, my daughter-in-law Amanda redirected our weekend plans by slipping rain boots on my three-year-old granddaughter's feet. She told Joy and me that, with all the rain puddles in the street, it was now time to do some "puddle stomping." Joy led the way as we walked the neighborhood, searching for rain puddles to stomp until we had splashed all the water out of them. Before we realized it, we both were laughing and hollering at the top of our lungs as water splashed everywhere. This was a moment of incredible joy shared with Joy that I will always cherish. This special time was all due to the wisdom of Joy's mother, who knew that joy can be found in many places. We must simply be willing to look for those places. Then we must choose to go to those places of joy when the pathway to the joy we were counting on is closed to us.

Into a world that believed joy was primarily a product of unilateral power and wealth, Jesus came and taught that joy is found in relational power and loving service. He taught that joy begins with a choice to love God, the fruit of which is loving and serving our neighbors. Sometimes pathways to joy through divine service are temporarily blocked by the pain of a tragic loss or an unwanted medical diagnosis. However, we must keep the faith with our eyes and ears open to the power of God's grace at work in the lives of the people around us. We can then discover another divine path that brings laughter, love, joy, and purpose into our lives, even amid life's unwanted interruptions. Therefore, I pray that you will attempt some "puddle stomping" with someone this week, bringing the joy of Christ into your heart and your relationship. In a world that needs more "puddle stompers," let us all do our part in "making the joyful noise" of splashing some water with a neighbor or, in my case, with my three-year-old granddaughter, who is rightly named *Joy*.

... when we **embrace** that, in the end,
God wins

> "And I heard a loud voice from the throne saying,
> 'Behold, the dwelling place of God is with humankind.
> God will dwell with them, and they will be his
> people. . . . God will wipe away every tear from their
> eyes, and death shall be no more, neither shall
> there be mourning, nor crying, nor pain anymore,
> for the former things have passed away.'"
>
> Revelation 21:3-4

An old preacher's story came to mind today, which I have heard repeated several times over the years. A group of seminary students was playing a pick-up game of basketball in the campus gym while a facilities manager was sitting in the stands with his Bible open. During a break, one of the players turned to the stands and asked, "What book of the Bible are you reading?" The man answered, "The book of Revelation." The seminarian was aware of how difficult Revelation is to understand, so he decided to test the facility manager's knowledge, anticipating that he would need to enlighten this individual with his own biblical prowess. So the seminarian asked, "What is the meaning of Revelation?" The facility manager paused and confidently answered, "Revelation has taught me that, in the end, God wins!" The seminarian nodded his head affirmatively and returned to the court.

The message of Easter (see the Gospel of John 3:16), and the book of Revelation (21:3-4) reveal that, in the end, God wins. When facing your own mortality or the mortality of someone you love, it is reassuring to know that death does not have the last word. Instead, the last word is "Christ is risen!" The last word is, "For God so loved the world, that he gave his only Son that whoever believes in him should not perish but have eternal life." The last word is, "God will dwell with us, and we will be his people. . . . God will wipe away every tear from our eyes, and death shall be no more." Thanks be to God for offering to us, through the crucified and risen Christ, the gifts of eternal love, hope, and joy. May we offer God's life-giving gift to others.

. . . when we have **loved ones** who **shield** us from **pitfalls**

"Even though I walk through the valley of the shadow of death, I will fear no evil, for you are with me; your rod and your staff they comfort me."

Psalm 23:4 ESV

When I arrived at my youngest son's home for a long weekend visit, I was greeted by Joy and Emogene, my three- and six-year-old granddaughters. After they walked me up the stairs to my room, Joy handed me a stuffed cheetah with which to sleep. Then six-year-old Emogene proceeded to issue a warning. "Now, Papaw," she began, "you do not want to dream while you're sleeping with the cheetah. If you do, you might dream that the cheetah sneaks up on you, bites you, and then eats you." After that heartfelt welcome by my granddaughters, accompanied by a foreboding warning, I reassured Emogene that I had no intention of dreaming while sleeping with the stuffed cheetah.

In the Old Testament story about David and his friend Jonathan (1 Samuel), Jonathan says to David, "Far be it from you! If I knew that it was determined by my father that harm should come to you, would I not tell you?" (1 Samuel 20:9 ESV). Those whom we love, we seek to protect and shield from harm. Knowing that we have people in our lives, like Emogene, who value us enough to protect us from the pitfalls of life, is reassuring and comforting. There is a peace that comes over us knowing we have loved ones with such compassion and knowing that God, our shepherd, is protecting us from harm with his rod and staff. This knowledge brings solace to our souls.

We experience many pitfalls in this life, like an unexpected cancer diagnosis or even a hungry cheetah that chooses to stalk us and threatens to chew us up and swallow us whole. Yet it is encouraging to know that we have a caring God, loving family members, and friends who are here for us to watch over us, warn us, and protect us. May we provide that same protection for others in harm's way.

...when we **take** the **time**
to **renew** our **souls**

> **"I will give you a new heart**
> **and put a new spirit in you."**
>
> Ezekiel 36:26 NIV

I am sitting here composing this *evotional* with a smile on my face and joy in my heart, having just returned from spending a weekend in Denver, Colorado, with my son Stephen and daughter-in-law Amanda. Since my aggressive cancer diagnosis, I have prioritized spending quality time with my family. This approach to living with cancer has resulted in an energizing renewal of my soul. I am now asking myself: "Why didn't I take more time before my diagnosis to proactively connect with my family and therefore connect with the Lord God who created us to be in community with one another?" Every time I have prioritized family connections, the outcome has been an incredible restoration of my soul.

For instance, Stephen and I golfed together this past weekend at the foot of a beautiful Colorado mountain range. We hiked into a Colorado state park, where we encountered the beauty of God's creation, including rock formations and a remarkable variety of colorful bird species. We saw the Colorado Rockies play the Atlanta Braves at the impressive Coors Field. We watched, together, one of our all-time favorite movies, *Glory,* and then enjoyed the nostalgia of watching the sequel to the first *Top Gun* movie. We visited about dad/son stuff and son/daughter-in-law/dad things throughout our busy weekend, letting each other know how much we love and respect each other. Sometimes we shared with words. Other times we communicated in silence, just enjoying the divine gift of being together in the moment.

During this past year, I have deliberately chosen to be with each member of my family in much the same way I was with Stephen and Amanda this past weekend. Trusting in the power of God's grace, I believe prioritizing time with my family has brought me to a point where I can honestly declare, "It is well with my soul."

How is it with your soul today? By God's grace and by choosing to prioritize spending time with your family, you will be able to confidently proclaim in good times and in not-so-good times, "It is well with my soul."

. . . when we embrace gratitude as our attitude

"We give thanks to you, Lord God Almighty, who is and who was, for you have taken your great power and begun to reign."

Revelation 11:17 ESV

When I was diagnosed with aggressive cancer over one year ago, I decided that I would spend what time I have left on this earth living with, rather than dying with, cancer. I chose from that moment forward to lean on the Lord God Almighty to help me make each day count. I prioritized spending time with family and friends and serving others through my ministry on the staff of St. Andrew. One of my sons encouraged me to identify people who energized and lifted me up and spend time with them. I followed his advice and found something in common with those who have repeatedly boosted my spirit. Each one of them has an "attitude of gratitude." For instance, on my one-year anniversary of battling cancer, I received this congratulatory note from one of my good friends who consistently lifts me up and gives me hope: "This is a huge deal . . . it's been a year, and I'm looking forward to congratulating you again next year at this same time."

This "attitude of gratitude" is a divine gift that Jesus himself embodied. Over the years, I have come to believe that one of the primary reasons Jesus attracted great crowds during his three years of ministry was that the people he encountered were lifted up by his grateful spirit. Jesus gave people hope. With many of the people he healed, he let them know he was grateful for their faith, which he credited with making them well. Jesus was thankful that the Lord God Almighty was present for him in the Garden of Gethsemane and on the cross. Jesus' last words from the cross to God were, "Father, into your hands I commit my spirit" (Luke 23:46 ESV). These words, for me, were a declaration of Jesus' gratitude that God would watch over him in the life to come, just as God had watched over him in this life.

I pray for you today that Christ's "attitude of gratitude" will reign supreme over your life. Furthermore, I pray that the gift of gratitude will lift you up and energize you to give others hope.

. . . when we **lift up** our **eyes** to gaze upon the **wonder** of **God's presence**

> "I lift up my eyes to the hills.
> From where does my help come?
> My help comes from the LORD,
> who made heaven and earth."
>
> Psalm 121:1-2 ESV

While battling cancer, I have had days that I have spent with my head lowered, engaged in a wrestling match with fear and anxiety. Yesterday was one of those days until I sat on my patio and looked up for a moment. A cloud in the shape of an angel floated across the bright blue sky, immediately drawing my attention. That heavenly cloud was followed by another in the shape of a small humming-bird. Then, another cloud in the form of a troll remind-ed me of the story of "Billy Goat Gruff." This troll cloud was followed by a seahorse that drifted quickly from one horizon to the next. While I contemplated the beauty and blessing of God's creation, my fear and worry floated away, replaced by emotions of awe and wonder. This sacred mo-ment was made possible because, by the grace of God, I chose to look up rather than down.

I imagine that, at the foot of the cross, the followers

of Jesus were looking downward due to their feelings of heartbreak, pain, and helplessness. Yet, if they had looked up for a moment, they would have experienced wonder and awe in the words of a dying Jesus who prayed on behalf of his executioners, "Father forgive them, for they know not what they do" (Luke 23:34 ESV). They would have heard Jesus empathically saying to a criminal being crucified next to him, "Today, you will be with me in paradise" (Luke 23:43 ESV). If they had chosen to lift their eyes to see and hear the grace-filled redemptive words of Jesus, the weight of their fear and anxiety would have been replaced by the joyful peace of God's awe and wonder.

My prayer is that you will pause today and lift your eyes to see and experience the awe and wonder of God's redemptive and joyful presence. Then I pray that you will choose to serve as an instrument of God's presence for someone who is downcast today.

. . . when we **celebrate** our **wins** in the midst of our **losses**

> **"Give thanks in all circumstances; for this
> is the will of God in Christ Jesus for you."**
>
> 1 Thessalonians 5:18 ESV

If I were to describe the defining characteristics of my immediate and extended family, I would include the word *competitive.* Due to the generosity of a close friend, my family and I had the opportunity to stay together for a week-long vacation on Kiawah Island, South Carolina.

When we got to the beach, we unpacked our boogie boards, and the competition began. We took the boards out into the ocean to catch waves. As soon as a good wave approached, we dropped down onto the board on our stomachs and rode the wave as far as possible toward the shore. I felt surprisingly good about the ten feet I traveled on a single wave until my sons and daughter-in- law covered somewhere between forty and fifty feet after catching the waves of their choice.

Now I might have had a moment when I sulked a little over my mediocre performance in relationship to the prowess of these youngsters. However, when I thought back to my terminal cancer diagnosis over a year ago, I stopped sulking and celebrated the fact that I was gifted with this extraordinary moment, playing on the beach with my family. This moment was a win for us all that was far beyond our comprehension over a year ago.

The Apostle Paul reminds us to give thanks in all circumstances. Over the years, I have argued with Paul's premise; however, I embrace his words today. My choice to accept his challenge has brought me great joy and peace.

I pray that you will find that same happiness by "giving thanks in all circumstances" and passing along your joy and peace to others.

... when we have significant goals to accomplish

"For even the Son of Man came not to be served but to serve, and to give his life as a ransom for many."

Mark 10:45 ESV

My wife, Sharon, and I have some significant health challenges, so setting a goal to take a family trip is no small matter. However, we decided that spending a week together with our family in a home on the beach was a goal well worth adopting and accomplishing. Once we decided we were going, I saw in Sharon a renewed energy and determination to increase her physical stamina. She exercised at the gym twice a week, took more frequent walks, and ate healthier foods. I rigorously followed my doctor's orders regarding medications and treatments that would help me be engaged and active during our family week at the beach. Words alone cannot adequately describe the outcome of our effort. Spending time at the beach with family was a phenomenal experience as we created memories that we will always cherish. Our focus on being victims of our aches and pains diminished significantly, replaced by the blessings of our love and deep gratitude for our wonderful family. What we discovered is that having a meaningful goal to accomplish brought us purpose, renewed energy, and tremendous joy.

Jesus himself modeled for us the importance of setting goals. In the Gospel of Mark, he clarified that his primary goal while walking this earth was not to be served but to serve. Furthermore, Jesus declared that he would be willing to give his life to help those in need. We know from Holy Scripture that Jesus honored and glorified God by fulfilling his divine goal and that his work brought him and those he served peace and fulfillment beyond all understanding. I pray that you will set aside time this week to create at least one crucial short-term and long-term goal for yourself. May accomplishing your goals, whether simple or epic, bring you renewed energy and incredible joy, and do the same for those you serve.

NOTE: This is the final *evotional* that Robert wrote.

The secret of a **life** of **faith**

Written by Arthur Jones

"Whoever finds their life will lose it, and whoever loses their life for my sake will find it."

Matthew 10:39 ESV

A month ago this Sunday, Robert's last *evotional* went out on the morning he took his last breath. I have missed the weekly emails with his unique Arkansas charm, can-do confidence, and humble faith. One of Robert's promises is that he would continue working on behalf of his God, Jesus Christ, until his very last breath. Friends—he did it. Robert showed us how to live, and he showed us how to die.

As a staff, we have debated what to do with his *evotionals.* We found only one answer: to make his beautiful, heartfelt words available to all who may benefit from his grace and wisdom.

God has called me now to fill the shoes of our beloved senior pastor of St. Andrew, but I am all too aware that I am not Robert Hasley. Yet I know I don't need to be. Just as Robert Hasley was different from his mentor Leighton Farrell, God has made us each unique for the moments to which we are called. This book helps us remember the time that was uniquely his, even while we prepare for the new time ahead.

As far as I can tell, the secret of a life of faith is to continue the mission of those who came before us in our own unique ways. As I write this, the work on foundations for the Hasley Chapel continues. This reminds me that the work of the church will never end. To honor Robert and the God he worshiped, we will continue with the same mission, passion, and love that allowed us to found this beautiful and faithful church community.

How are we going to lift up that mission moving forward? If we have breath and life, we still have something left on this earth to do for God. The amazing thing is that giving our lives to something larger than ourselves brings us new life over and over again.

Robert found more life in dying than any man I've ever met. How do we keep it going? What will it require of us?

We just need to remember that, when we give our lives to Christ, we know that everything is going to be all right. Everything is all right.

Scan to view our entire collection
of inspirational and devotional books
and other resources at Invite Resources.

Plano, Texas
inviteresources.com